Published by MTNWalker Media, L.L.C.
6080 South Hulen, Suite 360, PMB 101
Fort Worth, Texas 76132

AlexisFaere.com

ISBN 978-1-958786-10-9

Whispers of Love:
365 Wonder-Filled Prayers for Grandma

A Year of Delightful Conversations With God

Dedicated to my fun-loving Grandma...

Thank you for sharing these prayers with me, so that we could have a little time together each day.

Start anywhere in the book and use it every year to stay connected with each of your hearts.

Backward ...
(Forward...)

My Grandparents were gracious, loving people, and well-established in their traditional Christian beliefs. I saw many gaps between their 'way of life' and the lives of their Grandchildren, myself included.

For most of their lives, I lived far away from my Grandparents. As they began to age, and as more permanent daily care was required for them, there was a part of me that became distinctly aware of that distance. It was a distance that somehow longed for closer proximity. I felt deeply about the changes they were facing, and I wanted to be supportive and loving in the best way I knew how.

My creative approach to this life experience was to write a daily ditty, if you will, that would give my Grandparents, my Grandma and my Grandpa, a short moment of personal time with me each day. I wanted those moments to be filled with understanding, spark joy, to be fun, and be introspective. I wanted to invite them into my inner world in a way that they could experience and appreciate.

Being the traditional Christians that they were, how better to reach them than to propose a daily prayer? They, after all, were religious in their own daily devotional and prayer time. It was their 'language' and their rhythm.

It allowed me to lay a framework for us to be able to share with each other, to connect and in some way and respect one another in ways that we had not yet connected.

So, I set out to create a personal book for each of them, one for my Grandfather, and one for my Grandmother. The collection I'm offering here was the collection I offered to my Grandma.

Remember, this was written to be received by a person who had a belief system that was, shall we say, more stringent, perhaps, than my own. So, while the references to 'God', 'Savior', and so on, may not be your own personal favorite references, it is intended to be a prayer offered – however you may offer your own prayers, to whomever you may offer them.

Perhaps you've gifted this offering, as a Grandchild, to your own Grandmother. The point is that it is a moment of time, offered each day, for years on end, if wished; for a Grandchild to relate to a Grandparent in a kind, loving, supportive, and adventurous manner.

Enjoy these moments, and may your relationships grow and be blessed...

January 1

Our Heavenly Father,

We're starting a brand-new year today.
My Grandma's life is different now than it used to be.
Would you please watch over her?

Bless her day, today, and pave the way for the New Year
so that she finds at least 2 or 3 blessings in each day.

Please touch her heart in a way so she knows that she is
loved, and she is important – not only in our family but
also, in the families of those she touches each day.

January 2

God?

Grandma's house isn't in the same place where mine is.
I ask you to protect her today. Protect her house.

Watch over her as she makes her way
through the day today.
If she needs warmth, let her know warmth.

If she needs a fresh breeze, let her be aware of your
presence as you gently provide that breeze.
Thank you, for touching Grandma today.

January 3

Well God,

Today is a new day.
As Grandma experiences life today,
I'd really appreciate it if you would
let her know that I love her.

My soul sprouts with bright colors and splashes all
around because I'm a part of this wonderful Grandma.

Maybe some of those colors can splash
all the way to her heart.
Is that what makes rainbows?

I'm going to pretend there are
rainbows from my heart to hers –
all day long and through the night.

Thank you for color and splashes of joy!

January 4

Dear Lord,

You've touched my Grandma's life
every day that she has lived.
Thank you.

Before she was even my Grandma,
you led her through the experiences
that make her who she is today.
Thank you.

Thank you for opening my heart
so I can love my Grandma.

Peacefully...

January 5

Hello God. It's me!

Did you know that when I got up this morning
I thought about my Grandma?

I thought – I wonder
if she's drinking her coffee. I wonder if she's having
worship. I wonder if she's visiting with Grandpa.

I wonder if she's going to get her hair done today.
I wonder if she's talking with her friend today.

Thank you for the gift of this day.

January 6

Great healing and nurturing God,

Sometimes Grandma doesn't feel her best. As she
journeys through the days when she's not quite up to par,
I wonder if you could envelop her with your cradling and
nurturing hands. Even grandmas like to be held.

She cared enough to hold me once when I didn't feel so
good – I'd like to know that Grandma is cared for, too.

Thank you for nurturing Grandma.

January 7

God?

You know when your sunshine feels
like a blanket of warmth?

Could you help Grandma to feel that
cuddly warmth sometime today?

Sometimes the days are rather cold,
and that sunshine warmth surely
does a body good.

Here's a warm hug from me to Grandma.
Thanks for helping her to feel my hugs.

Warmly...

January 8

Glorious Lord,

What an amazing thing you do each day – creating new days with sunrises and sunsets. Your art upon the heavens is surely a blessing. I like the way you make it so that Grandma and I both have a sky to behold, and yet each one is different.

I'm sure the sky I behold today is a very different-looking sky to Grandma.

May your heavenly art bestow upon her a feeling of hope, and may she sense the love of her family through this day.

Amazed...

January 9

It's me again God.

Thank you for being there every day, Lord. I'm comforted to know that you're always watching over Grandma – that way she's never alone.

It is my prayer, Dear Lord, that Grandma feels your presence in whatever way is best for her today.

You're constant and sure...

January 10

Dear God,

Have you ever just laughed because you are full of joy?

Joy is such a happy word. Joy, joy, joy!

I say it over and over and in myself,
I can feel my insides start to wiggle.

Joy, joy, joy, joy, joy!
Soon my wiggle turns into a giggle
I can barely contain.
Wiggle, giggle, joy, joy, joy!

Thank you for joy.

January 11

God,

Did you know that my Grandma is an amazing woman? She has loved in ways that are truly amazing for human people (and she's a wonderful human people)!

Thank you for the many ways you lead Grandma to express love and thank you for the many ways you open people's hearts so her love can be felt and experienced.

Thank you for the amazing woman that is my Grandma. Vibrantly...

January 12

Dear Heavenly Father,   Quietly...

January 13

Hey God,

You must really enjoy watching over our lives. I say that because you give us flowers and critters and other people for us to share our lives with.

Grandma is always generous when she shares herself with me. I thank you, Grandma.

God Bless our lives today!

January 14

Tender and Loving God,

You made our eyes so that we could see, and so
that we could cry and so that we can laugh.

I know sometimes I cry, and your hand is there to guide
me through the life that happens when I cry.

When Grandma cries, will you let her know that her
tears are crystal blessings that help life to unfold?

Thank you for your comfort.

January 15

Let's have a talk, God.
(Thank you for talking.)

We have so many ways to talk with each other.
Thank you for the telephone, the letters, the visits, and
conversations that grace my Grandma's life.

Thank you, God, for talking with us, and listening
with us, so that we might learn more about
who we are in your world.

I enjoy talking with you about Grandma.

Thank you for mouths.

January 16

Okay God.

We've started on our journey for this New Year.

Walk with my Grandma as her days unfold and
her life blossoms with gifts from you.

Walk with her today where she roams and when she
rests continue to shower her with love.

Help her to recognize 3 gifts from you today.

Abundantly...

January 17

Wow!

Grandma loves me. God, you are indeed exuberant. Your gracious love reaches out and touches me through the loving gestures of my Grandma.

She took time to have tea parties with me when I was just a little one; she took me on camping trips; she let me play the piano for her; and she always says a prayer for me each day.

Thank you for all the ways Grandma says I love you.

Exuberantly...

January 18

Psssst! God!

On this day, could you guide someone to touch Grandma's hand so that she knows your presence?

Today is another day in Grandma's life and I'd really like it if you could open her heart to something really special today.

Thanks, God.

January 19

How long has it been since Grandma remembered
something really fun she did as a child?

Could you spark a memory that
fills her heart with laughter?

Grandma could use a good giggle today.
I like the way giggles express your joy.

Thank you for the way our hearts tickle when we giggle.

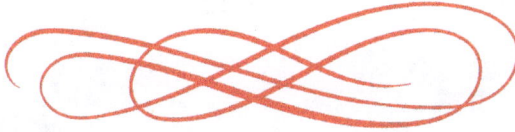

January 20

Bountiful Savior,

Thank you for providing a place for
Grandma to call home.

I'm glad she has shelter, a warm bed to sleep
in at night, and a place to hang her hat.

As Grandma makes her journey through this day,
help her to know that her home is a blessing
and that you care about her.

Graciously...

January 21

For food, we are grateful Dear Lord.

You have always found a way to provide
for my Grandma through her life.

As she nourishes her body with food and
nutrients, nourish her soul so that she
knows of your wondrous and guiding love.

When her belly is full, help her heart
to feel nourished as well.
Amen.

January 22

Wondrous Father,

This thing you give us, we call it a mind,
thank you for it. We can think, we can
remember, we can figure out something
about your purpose in every day.

Thank you for Grandma's mind.

When you see the time is right, could
you let her see me giving her a hug –
just so she knows that her
mind is good and kind.

I ask this in your name...

January 23

Dear God,

You know that Grandma loves Grandpa.
When Grandma spends time with Grandpa, whether in her heart or in person, help her to understand your wondrous and gracious gifts.

Thank you for the many blessings Grandma has because she shares her life with Grandpa.

I know this is part of what makes Grandma who she is today.

Thank you.

January 24

Brrrrrrrrr!

I feel that cold breeze!

When Grandma feels a chill, could
you also help her feel something
warm – in her heart, on her hands,
wrapping her body to
keep her warm?

Help her to know that warmth
is full of love from me to her.

Thank you, God.

January 25

Guiding Father,

Your always-present grace watches
over us all. As you watch over
Grandma today, help her to
be thankful for friends.

Friends are grace-full.
Thank you for all the friends that
touch my Grandma's life.

Gracefully...

January 26

God of Life,

Sometimes our days are just
ordinary days.

I like that it is ordinary for me to
have a Grandma that loves me –
and that she has a Grandchild
that loves her.

Thank you for what helps life to
seem ordinary.

Deliciously...

January 27

Oh, Dear God,

For family we are grateful.

With families,
we have the opportunity to
grow our hearts and our selves.

We're fortunate to have
the family we have.

Thank you for the Grandma I have.

Thank you for right now!

January 28

God?

Did you hear Grandma singing?
She was singing a nice tune.

You know that music fills her heart
with life that is good.

Thank you for music that Grandma hears and sings.
Thank you for the way you speak to us through music.

Listening...

January 29

Our Father,

who art in Heaven, hallowed be thy name.
Thy kingdom come, thy will be done,
on earth as it is in heaven.

Give us this day, our daily bread, and
forgive those who aren't always kind to us.
Lead us not into temptation and deliver us from evil.

For Thine is the Kingdom,
the Power, and the Glory forever. Amen.

January 30

Father,

Thank you for letting Grandma
hear our prayers for her.

She is an amazing person – this
woman that I call Grandma.

Help her to feel fulfilled as she
says her blessings today.

Prayerfully...

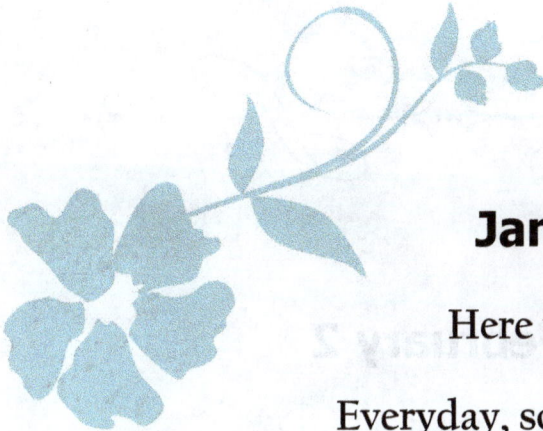

January 31

Here we go, Lord.

Everyday, someone special has
said a prayer for Grandma.

Whatever she needs, whatever
she's wanting, could you just let
her know of your guiding presence?

Let an angel fill her heart today, and let
angels go with her wherever she goes.

Watchfully...

February 1

Hello, Lord Jesus.

You know it's probably been a while since
Grandma thought of a teacher in her life.

As she remembers a teacher that touched her,
let us all remember the teachers we have in each day.

We're learning, Lord.

February 2

God,

There's a deer in the woods and it seems like
your little creature could use a hand.

Touch your creatures today, and guide them
through the life that is meant to be theirs today.

With wonder...

February 3

A quick thought, Oh Lord.

I love Grandma.

You're awesome!

February 4

Dear God,

I think Grandma could use your help today.

I don't know what goes on right now, but Grandma's heart could use a little burst of your love and guidance.

When I see the stars tonight, I'll thank each one for guarding and guiding.

Sleeping with angels...

February 5

Well God,

I know how comfy it is when I lay my head on a pillow
at night, when I'm tired and ready for rest.

Well, I was wondering if you could help Grandma
know that comfy feeling today.

Knowing my Grandma is there helps me to
feel comfy about who and what I am.

Grandma snuggles...

February 6

Heavenly Father and Creator,

Thank you for the creation of this day and for allowing me to enjoy days with my Grandma.

In the creation of this day, thank you, too, for creating blessings for us to discover.

Discovering blessings...

February 7

Dear God,

It's February now.

The year is moving right along.

As Grandma's year continues to unfold, let her soul understand that our souls love her dearly.

Help this year to continue to be full of blessings.

Thank you, Lord.

February 8

Powerful and Loving God,

In as much as we know so very little about
you, we know little about ourselves.

Today, would you guide Grandma so she
learns something about herself today?

May what she learns be enriching to her dear life.

Searching...

February 9

Wondrous Lord,

Icicles fill me with wonderment.

They are cold and seemingly destructive
and at the same time, they melt and
change the life they surround.

You are always there, surrounding us and protecting us.

Thank you for your watchful eye.

Bewildered...

February 10

God,

When Grandma remembers a special memory today,

help her to know how special she is, too.

Grandma is like a special place for me.

When I'm with her, I joy in the

life she shares with me

and the life she has

shared with others.

When I am with her in my heart,

my soul is richly blessed.

Specialness...

February 11

Eh hmm. God?

When Grandma thinks of her family today, help her to remember something about each one that helps her to smile.

When Grandma smiles, it's like biting into a freshly baked loaf of bread – it's refreshing and nourishing.

Smiling...

February 12

Hello God.

Today a feather swooped down and touched my face.

I remember when Grandma used to tickle my nose with her finger.

I think that feather was Grandma's gentle touch – encouraging me on my way.

For Grandma's gentle touches, thank you Dear Lord.

February 13

Amazing and Graceful God,

Thank you for the rest that Grandma had last night.

Thank you for watching over her so that she could
wake up refreshed and ready for this new day.

Thank you for protecting her from harm
and for showering her life with Grace.

Creatively...

February 14

Good morning God!

Thanks for that bright, beaming sunshine you give us.

It's good to know that your bright light is there,
even when clouds color our skies.

When I see and feel this sunshine, I imagine that it
reaches out and touches my Grandma,
and shines on her home, filling her
with warmth and hope.

Adventurously...

February 15

Oh, Dear God,

This morning, I just woke up on the wrong side of the bed!

Is there really a wrong side of the bed?

Anyway, I would imagine that Grandma has those kinds of days too.

When she does, would you smile upon her and let her know that it's okay to have a wrong-side-of-the-bed day?

Perplexed...

February 16

It's me, God.

Grandma taught me to crochet.

One of my favorite comfy times is when I'm snuggled under the blanket she knitted for me – it's as if she has her arms wrapped around me gently holding my soul and life.

If you could find a moment to hold Grandma in your presence in such a way, I would surely appreciate that.

Warmly...

February 17

It's a little thing, God –

Ice cream is such a special treat. When I am aware of my Grandma, like I am today, it's like a refreshing dish of ice cream. Sweet thoughts are delicious moments for the soul. Thank you for this delicious moment.

Discovering....

February 18

Heavenly Father,

As we experience that day-to-day feeling, help Grandma to find rejoicing in aging. If we didn't age, we might not ever find the time to say a daily prayer for grandmas.
I like this part of aging.

Thank you for the gifts of aging!

February 19

For grains and fruits, for soup and salad, for candy corn and peppermints... Dear Lord, we give you thanks.

For a Grandma who cares, who loves, and who prays, thank you, Dear Lord.

February 20

Dear God,

My Grandma is such an inspiring woman.

Who inspires her?
As she travels through this day,
would you please inspire
Grandma in some way?

She inspires me and I thank you for the ways you open my heart to be inspired by her.

Inspiringly...

February 21

Ouch! God!

My heart has an ouchy!

Sometimes life is not as gentle as I think it should be.

I know when my heart aches you're there,
but it's hard for me to remember that
you are there and I'm growing.

When Grandma has a heart ouchy, could you shower
her with awareness that you're there to help?

Authentically...

February 22

Dear Father in Heaven,

Grandma's soothing hands have touched my life in so many varied ways. Thank you for the soothing way you touch Grandma's life each day.

When a soothing hand embraces my Grandmother, I hope she remembers that your embracing spirit is at work in her life.

Supportingly...

February 23

Surprise God!

When you blanket our world with snow, the day is new and fresh with surprises.

It's kind of like waking up one day and realizing that there's a Grandperson out there who loves their Grandma.

Refreshingly...

February 24

Blessed Lord,

I feel angry sometimes.
Is it possible that Grandma feels angry too?

After I feel angry, I can calm down and
always find ways to learn from the angry feelings.

When Grandma feels angry, could you enlighten her
in some way so she, too, can learn about herself?

When she learns and shares, I learn.
Thanks for the way anger can teach us about ourselves.

Stretching...

February 25

Hey God,

I was wondering about something.

When I feel love for my Grandma, can she feel that?

I believe that I can feel it when she loves me.

When that happens, it's like the Grandma pocket in my heart just spills over and touches other parts of me.

Help Grandma to feel it when I love her.

Curiously...

February 26

Mighty Father,

Sometimes I have days that just taste bad –
I just would rather that didn't happen.

But, when the day is over and another day
is journeyed, the day that tasted bad
seems to invite my heart to grow.

When Grandma has a day that doesn't taste
so great, can her heart be invited to grow, too?

Experimenting...

February 27

Good and Gracious God,

Goodness is surely one of your generous gifts.

Sharing my heart with Grandma has only
enriched the goodness I feel with her.

I hope Grandma feels goodness today.

Sagaciously...

February 28

God... Is two-in-one day too many?

In years when we're leaping, is it okay to have
two prayers for Grandma in one day?

One prayer would be that Grandma
enjoys her nap today.

Another prayer would be that
Grandma smiles today.

February 29

Father in Heaven,

What are your thoughts about leaping?

What about this leap of faith that you
challenge us with?

One leap of faith that I experience is
when I share with Grandma
about who I am.

The leap is in having faith that
she will still love me.

Whatever Grandma's leap of faith is,
could you guide her with that today?

Leaping...

March 1

Wow God!

It's March already.

What surprises will this month bring
to Grandma in her year this year?

Whatever treasures of life are in store
for her, please let her discover
the blessings in each one.

Progressively...

March 2

Dear Father,

There is a miracle in my life today.

Grandma is aware that her
Grandones journey through life
with Grandma in their hearts.

It feels like a miracle that we can
share in life with each other this way.

Whatever miracle Grandma might
experience today, let it deepen
and enrich her life.

Miraculously...

March 3

Hello God?

Are you there? Are you really there?
Life is always so full of change,
and I know change is a blessing.

But, sometimes it's hard to remember that you're there.

If Grandma is having trouble remembering that
you're there, could you send her a gentle reminder?

Faithfully...

March 4

Father above,

You know how you gently let us know that
the seasons are going to change?

Maybe it's a day that really feels like spring, or smells
like spring – but spring hasn't quite sprung yet?

As Grandma's life continues to change, could
you give her a gentle nudge and let her
know that you're right
there in her heart?

Thank you.

March 5

Dear God,

I saw that bird soaring through your grand universe the other day. When I see a bird soaring, I'm reminded of how vast your universe is, and how small my part of it seems.

If there is any way for Grandma to feel my love for her in a way that is vast like your universe, I'd like that for her.

Expressively...

March 6

Pssst! God!

How refreshing it is when we take naps.

I like nap time because my soul is free to play
and my body is nourished.

When Grandma takes a nap today, open the door
for her to enjoy some good soul play.

Playfully...

March 7

God,

Is it possible that Grandma could have a day without pain?

If pain is part of her journey, could you help her heart understand what the pain is teaching her?

Maybe it's physical pain, maybe it's a pain in her soul, and maybe it's a pain of routine.

Help Grandma to understand more about her pain today.

 Inquiringly...

March 8

Dear Lord,

That Grandma is able to enjoy
something about today, I am grateful.

Thank you, too, for the pleasure
that comes with enjoyment.

Thank you for the pleasure
of my Grandma!

Amen.

March 9

Glorious and Mighty Father,

Sunrise this morning, the birth of a new day, the birth
of something wonderful in my Grandma's world.

The rich and glowing brightness of the
energy you give us with the sun.

May sunrise happen in Grandma's life today.

Energetically...

March 10

Loving Lord,

Sometimes we are faced with challenges that we'd rather not deal with. If Grandma has such a challenge in her life, could you help her know that the challenge is life enriching in some way? Help her to understand that challenges can be blessings.

Reaching...

March 11

Lord,

Sometimes it seems that each day is just the same old thing: the same old routine; the same old people; the same old food. When Grandma has a case of the "same old stuff" could you throw something in there so her "same old world" is a little different?

Refreshingly...

March 12

Maybe Dear God.

Maybe she's in her chair resting.

Maybe she's over at a friend's house to enjoy something freshly baked.

Maybe she's just looking out the window, wondering how her day will be.

Maybe she's aware that I love her and that she's really special to me.

Whatever it is for Grandma today, thank you Dear Lord.

March 13

Lord, I gotta know something.

Does Grandma still get any tickley feelings on the inside because she's really excited about something?

Does Grandma still feel like clapping her hands and singing a happy song?

Does Grandma still feel like the little girl that just got a new doll for Christmas?

What do you think, Lord?

March 14

Gracious Father,

Thank you for the many ways you provide for Grandma.

Especially, thank you for providing her with a family that cares about her.

Abundantly...

March 15

Awesome Father,

I know that Grandma is always doing things for
people that make her seem like she's an angel.

She is an angel unaware when she says prayers for her
loved ones (troubled and untroubled),
an angel unaware
when she married Grandpa and mothered
children that weren't of her,
an angel unaware
when she helps Grandpa eat his hamburgers.

Bless this angel unaware!

March 16

God,

One thing about the chaos of dust – it always settles.
When our lives seem chaotic, there also comes
a time when that dust settles too.

It seems that when dust settles,
it somehow makes a home for itself.

I hope that some of the chaos that
Grandma has
will find a home today.

Thoughtfully...

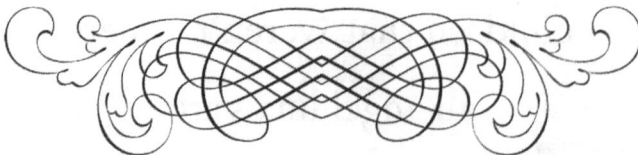

March 17

Fun One,

Today we're celebrating the color green.

Is Grandma wearing green?

She better wear something green 'cuz
she might get pinched if she gets caught without it.

I don't want anyone to pinch my Grandma –
quick help her find some green!

Little green men...

March 18

Hello God,

I remember what it feels like after Grandma's
Thanksgiving dinner and we're all ready for a nap,
just before the football game.

That is such a fulfilling experience – full tummies, family
fellowship, time out to be aware of what we're thankful for.

Anyway could we wake up the feeling in Grandma today?

Calm...

March 19

Wise and Wonderful Father,

Did you know that Grandma is a library?

She has so many life experiences that
we could just open up our own place
for people to come and read or learn.

For Grandma's wisdom and experience,
I thank you.

Open...

March 20

Remember, God?

Remember when I used to take a walk
with Grandma after dinner?

Well, her little body doesn't do those kinds
of walks anymore, but in my heart I still walk with her.

Walk with Grandma today, and let her know
that I'm walking with her too.

Step-by-step...

March 21

God of Wonder,

I see Grandma's magic!
She's magic because she knows
how to have a tea party.

She's magic because she can sit down
and play the piano without music.

She's magic because she's your child.

Magically...

March 22

God?

When Grandma reads me stories,
I feel enchanted.

Today when Grandma reads this
prayer, I hope she feels enchanted.

Embrace...

March 23

Dear Lord,

Does Grandma still draw pictures?

If you could help her find a way to draw a

picture today, I think she would enjoy that.

When she's finished with her picture,

I hope she puts in on her refrigerator.

Then, when she looks at the picture,

she can smile.

Creatively...

March 24

Sweet Jesus,

We've talked a little bit about family.

Thank you for the family we have because of our origin and thank you for the family we have because it's a choice to consider them family.

You know, like Aunt Ruth.

Thank you for Grandma's family – kinfolk and others!

March 25

Well, God –

The way it seems our life works, Grandma has a whole lot more years under her belt than I do.

If I get the pleasure of being a Grandma someday, I hope that I can contribute to my Grandchildren's lives the way Grandma contributes to mine.

Giving...

March 26

Dear Lord,

...the rest is easy.

March 27

Tell me, God.

When was the last time Grandma read a book out loud?

Isn't there a little book that Grandma could
read out loud to herself today?

When she reads to herself, I wonder if it is possible for
her to hear herself and feel nurtured by that?

Studying...

March 28

Oh Dear Jesus,

Did you see that dream that Grandma had last night?

Dreaming is like giving our minds a chance to play.

Whatever Grandma's dream is tonight,
maybe she'll discover a kind of surprise somehow.

Renewing...

March 29

Good God,

Like deserts after a good meal, life has

desert moments, too. Today I hope that

Grandma gets a candy corn somewhere in

her life – a nice little sweetness

that soothes and encourages.

Respectfully...

March 30

God of life,

One of the special moments I like to think about

is when I saw Grandma kissing Grandpa

(or Grandpa kissing Grandma).

I'm glad my Grandparents kiss,

they surely love each other.

Their kisses teach me fun and

special ways to express love.

Endearlingly...

March 31

Dear God,

Does Grandma really realize how important it is to be who she is? I'd like for her to know how important she is to me, and how important she is to everyone who knows her. Grandma is very important.

Grace-full-ly...

April 1

Dear Jesus,

Does Grandma ever write letters to you? Letters to you don't have to be very long, just a line or two.

If Grandma would like to write you a letter, maybe she could jot it down and put it under a pillow.

Then when she rests on that pillow, your angels will be there to take care of her.

Resting with Angels...

April 2

God?

It's one of your children,

Sometimes I have a day and I just feel crabby.
When I feel crabby nothing seems to go right.

If Grandma has a crabby day, could you help
her remember that you still love her, even when
it's hard for her to remember that?

Thank you for loving Grandma when she's crabby.

April 3

Delightful and Kind Spirit,

I have a dream that someday I will touch a life
and somehow help that life to be free and fly.

What are Grandma's dreams? What does she hope for?

Maybe Grandma could write down a dream
of hers and put it in a teacup.

Then when you see fit, I wonder if you would guide
her through, helping her dream to come true.

Hope-full-ly...

April 4

Creative Father,

Does Grandma ever feel silly?

Silly is such a good feeling.

Maybe there's a way that Grandma could feel
silly – in the kindest sort of way.

Maybe when she's silly, she can let a giggle
come out – maybe even giggle out loud.

Whimsical...

April 5

Mmmmmmmmm.

Potato soup.

Not just any potato soup – Grandma's potato soup.

Gentle Jesus, when Grandma says a blessing for a meal she has today, I'd really like it if you could give her the feeling of Grandma's good potato soup in her belly.

April 6

Dear God,

Today I'm remembering how gentle my Grandma is.

Any Grandma, who is a Great-Grandma, which allows herself to be called Grandma Grape surely must be a gentle Grandma.

Remember how gentle Grandma Grape is.

April 7

Heavenly Father,

Once when I was hurt,
Grandma loved me anyway.

That's the way of your love.
If Grandma is hurting in some way,
could you let her know that I love her?

Let her know the way of your love.

Caring...

April 8

Father God,

Grandma's life is like a treasure chest.
When I discover new things about her,
it's like finding a genuine treasure.

Thank you for all the treasures that come
with this person that is my Grandma.

Passionately...

April 9

Artistic God,

That flower that is about to bloom is a gift.

I think when Grandma wakes up today,
she will be like that flower that is
almost ready to bloom.

When she blooms, let her life be
full of fragrance and color.

Pleasure...

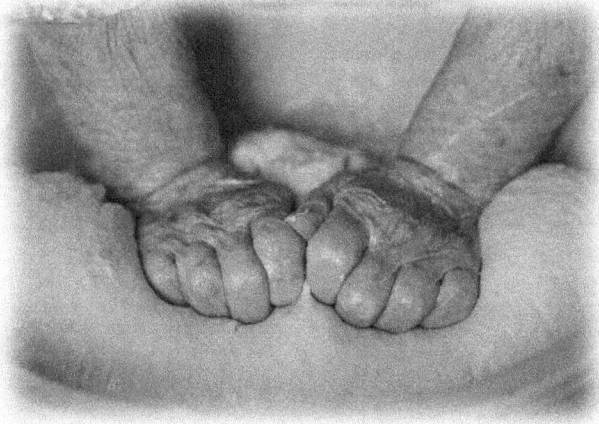

April 10

You know, God,

Grandma never had tons and tons of money.
But you know, she's always managed to
have enough when she needed it.

Thank you for the wealth that you provide so that
Grandma has what she needs, when she needs it
(and a little extra for frivolous spending on occasion).

Thank you... Grand Provider.

April 11

Hello God,

I noticed the other day that my Grandma is very courageous.

She must get courage from you, because it seems so unwavering.

Thank you for the gift of courage that you bless Grandma with.

When she requires courage, would you keep it strong for her?

Blessings...

April 12

Guardian Lord,

I'm not sure what Grandma has in store for her day today.

If she is traveling from one place to another, I would ask that you provide her with traveling kindnesses.

Bless her travels so that she might know of your presence.

Caring...

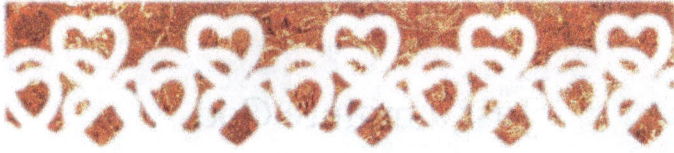

April 13

It's time for a celebration, God!

Do you remember that you made a wonderful gift today,

perhaps any given day?

Her name is Grandma (to me)
and perhaps others know her by other names!

With the caring love you used when you created her,
may that same caring love help her to know
that she is one of your wonderful children.

I'm glad Grandma was born!

April 14

Just a minute God,

You are so patient and affectionate God.

Sometimes we just need that extra minute to take care

of whatever life is happening at any given moment.

If Grandma needs an extra minute for something

today, help her to know that your

gifts of patience and affection are with her.

Momentarily...

April 15

Dear Jesus,

Our government helps us sometimes. I know that it has helped my Grandma on more than one occasion.

Sometimes, though, it seems the government is not such a wonderful organization.

On this day that we all pay our taxes, let us be thankful for the government and the provisions therein.

Abundantly...

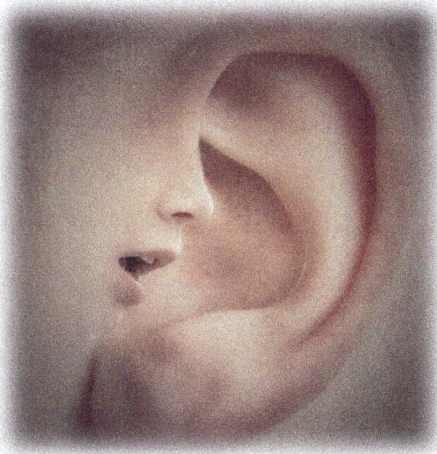

April 16

Yes Lord?

Grandma's listening to your sound and steady direction...

April 17

Hey God,

Splish splash!

Bath time feels so good

to the skin and muscles.

Not only does the water cleanse our

bodies, oh how it symbolically gives

us a chance to clean our souls, too.

When Grandma takes a bath today,

refresh and clean her heart, too.

Exhilarating...

April 18

Gracious Heavenly Father,

Being alive is a remarkable thing.

I like feeling very alive in my day-to-day existence.

I wonder if you could help Grandma

to really feel alive today.

Help her to feel in some way that she

is glad that she is alive today.

Remarkably...

April 19

Wow Jesus. Free spirits.

What a joyous feeling that we can allow our spirits to be free.

If Grandma is having a hard time with freeing part of her spirit, could you help encourage her to make a choice to practice freedom?

Freely...

April 20

Father,

It seems that many times we have a place
for everything – that everything fits
into a box somehow.

Sometimes what my heart needs is to
explore outside the box a little bit.

If Grandma could use an out-side-the-box
awareness today, usher that awareness for her.

Marvelously...

April 21

Dear Father,

What would we ever do without friends?

I like friends.

I thank you that Grandma has friends
to share her life with.

Sometimes Grandma is just the friend I want and need.

I suspect her friends feel the same way.

Thank you for Grandma's friends.

April 22

You know, God,

We've been having these daily chats
for a good long while now.

I'm reminded of guest books.

When you touch our lives with gifts and blessings,
it's like having you sign the guest book of our life.

Thanks for signing Grandma's guest book, everyday.

GRRRRrrrrrrrrrrrrrrrrrrrrrrrrrr
GRRRRLLLLLLLLLLLLLLLLLLLLLLLLL

April 23

Kind Father,

Sometimes we make the choice to feel angry.
Angry is such an interesting feeling.
Sometimes it feels destructive and evil;
yet other times it feels full of energy.

I'm just sure that Grandma feels angry sometimes.
When she does, please help her to understand
her choices and help her to use the energy
of anger in a way that grows her spirit.

Exasperation...

April 24

Loving Father,

Each day we are faced with little things
that we choose to endure.

Endurance is something we build and look for.

Whatever it is that Grandma might be
enduring today, it is my prayer
that she knows you're there with her.

Courageously...

April 25

Playful Christ,

I saw one of your lightening bugs today.

What a marvelous inspiration.
That beings come into our lives
unexpectedly and light our way.

Grandma has done this for me on many occasions.

Keep sending beings along the way
to meet up with Grandma.

Grandmas need lightening bugs too you know.

Buzzing...

April 26

But God...

Sometimes I feel like an orphan.

I know that there are people in my life

that love and care for me.

But today it is hard for me to feel that

compassion for some reason.

Open my soul so that I know that when I am

feeling orphaned, I'm aware of your presence.

Longing...

April 27

God of all Creation,

Cats and dogs are a fine creation.

How many times Grandma has been blessed
with a kitten or a puppy in her life.

Grandma is like a kitty to me sometimes.

She purrs and she snuggles, and she likes
it when I'm there.

When Grandma thinks of cats or dogs today,
help her to purr inside.

Listening...

April 28

Healing Lord,

I imagine that when something inside me heals,
it also heals something in Grandma.

When Grandma is healing, send an angel to be with her.

Gently...

April 29

Renewing Father...

Naps are revitalizing.

When Grandma naps today, make her home a nap zone.

Fill her home with goodness as she naps
and fill her body with whatever it needs.

Resting...

April 30

Well God,

I just didn't feel like doing it!

When I procrastinate,
I'm not aware of the
wonders of completion.

When Grandma procrastinates,
help her to know that it's okay,
and wake up the miracle of
completion.

When the time is right...

May 1

First things first, God!

Grandma is loved.

I love Grandma.
Lots of people... love Grandma.

Hugs...

May 2

Lord and Savior,

There are days when I need to be saved from myself.

When I listen, you send someone to
help me get outside myself.

When Grandma needs to be saved from herself,
be there for her... or send someone her way.

Illuminating...

May 3

So how are we doing God?

Goodness gracious how the days
in this year have flown by!

It's May already.

Even though it may seem that this day is flying by,
I hope Grandma sees a flower today, and remembers
that she is on a journey that shapes and
molds this year of her life.

Awareness...

May 4

God,

When Grandma goes to sleep at the end
of this day, fill her cottage with angels
that watch over her and her home.

Let the angels be full of life and safeness.

Patiently...

May 5

Hello God?

Are you there?

Hello! It's one of your children –

Are you there? Hello.

Is anybody home? God, are you there?

I know you're there somewhere!

When Grandma needs you,
let her know that you're there.

Searching...

May 6

Nurturing Father,

This crunchy lettuce tastes so good!

That orange carrot is tasty, too.
Mmmmm, that tomato is sweet and juicy.
Oooooh that tart pickle – gives me pucker power!

For the food that Grandma eats today, I thank you.

May 7

Merciful Jesus,

There are lots of people in this world
that forget about their grandmas.

Every single day I enjoy knowing
that I know my Grandma.

I hope she feels like she's a person
deserving of respect and honor.

With enduring spirit...

May 8

Almighty Father,

I know you know that Grandpa told me

that he loves Grandma very much.

What a wonderful gift it is that I have had

opportunities to share in knowing

just how much he loves her.

I imagine that when Grandpa dies,

he'll still love Grandma whole bunches!

Wow!

May 9

Beautiful Savior,

It's that glorious time of year when things are vibrant with color and sleeping plants are showing definite signs of life.

As Grandma wakes from her rest today, may she know that she's growing in the light of your guidance.

Vivaciously...

May 10

Father God,

Today I light a candle in hopes that the energy of the graceful and royal flame would also dance in the heart of my Grandma.

You know what a dancing candle flame is like; that's what it feels like to have Grandma in my heart.

Glowing...

May 11

Hey Father,

You know how sometimes a soda is just what
your taste buds are thirsty for?

Then when you drink that soda it just quenches
the thirst that you longed for?

Whatever it is that Grandma thirsts for today,
I hope you can provide something that will
quench the thirst just right!

Expectantly...

May 12

God,

Do you ever write letters?

When the time is right,
would you write a letter to Grandma
and share with her a glimpse of your generous grace?

Glimmering...

May 13

Wheeee God!

I was out in the spring rain yesterday
and found a bit of a mud puddle.

I took my shoes off and wiggled my
toes in the mud.

What a great young feeling that is!

When was the last time Grandma
squished mud between her toes?

Dare she try it again some day?

Squishy mud!

May 14

Dear Holy God,

I have a prayer pocket I use to remember
people who want a special
prayer now and then.

Today my Grandma is in my prayer pocket.

God love Grandma real good!

May 15

Surprise Father!

Life is full of surprises and undiscovered treasure.
Grandma may be undiscovered to some folks,
but she is hidden treasure to me.

Revealing...

May 16

Knowledgeable Lord,

You've touched my Grandma's heart very deeply
and you know all about her.

However, she needs to be touched today.

Open her heart so she can receive your blessings.

Thank you, Lord.

May 17

God of Joy?

Does Grandma remember a day when
there were lots of balloons?

Today I imagine Grandma's life filled with brightly
colored balloons – each one filled with a joy about her life.

Past, present, future...

May 18

Thanks God!

I just love the way Grandma's house smells.

I know when I step into the door, I'm in the right place.

Today I wish for Grandma that she knows

she's in the right place.

That's all.

May 19

Watchful One,

I have a cat in my lap right now.

I think cats are angels with paws.

I know Grandma loves cat creatures too!

If she doesn't have a real cat in her lap, I wonder if you could help her feel like she does anyway.

Purrrrrfectly...

May 20

Ominous Father,

I behold the great ocean as if it is a powerful symphony – everything carefully orchestrated.

I feel the same way sometimes when I behold the many ways my Grandma loves me and the ways I love her.

I hope Grandma feels that today.

May 21

Jesus loves her, this I know;
for the Bible tells me so.

Grandmas,

Grandchildren

one and all, we are thankful for it all.

May 22

Oh, God!

I feel so foolish today!

Does Grandma ever feel foolish
about something she's said or done?

Your bountiful grace cradles me
when I feel foolish.

When Grandma feels foolish, could
you cradle her in your grace?

Wondering...

May 23

Father,

Grandma is a gift from God.

She blesses my life with snuggly things, with her open arms, with her candy jar, with her love, with herself.

Thanks for Grandma gifts.

May 24

Hurry God,

Send Grandma a messenger.

The message I have for her is that she is resourceful.

Refreshingly...

May 25

Marvelous Father,

Today I walked in the green grass barefoot.

It's a fresh and rejuvenating thing to
wiggle my toes in your soft grass.

Does Grandma ever wiggle her toes in your grass?

Spritefully...

May 26

Honorable Heavenly Father,

In the town where my Grandma lives,

flags are displayed on Memorial Day.

She speaks with respect about those who've

served our country as she enjoys the beauty

of regal and stately flying flags.

By raising a family, it seems to me that Grandma

has served her country, too.

Respectfully...

May 27

Ever Present God,

Is there a special friend in
Grandma's life – someone she is
suddenly remembering today?

Maybe it's a friend from her
childhood. Maybe it's a friend she
had when she first got married.

Whoever her friend is,
I hope these are enriching
thoughts for her.

Constantly...

May 28

Jesus,

Grandma is looking for something.

Would you be so kind as to help her find it?

I know she'll say thank you.

Discovering...

May 29

Generous Father,

Does Grandma ever ask for your forgiveness?

If she does, I hope you will respond abundantly.

Whatever it is that Grandma seeks forgiveness for,
I hope you can ignite her soul with blessing.

Setting it free...

May 30

Yes God?
... I'm listening...

May 31

Dear Creator,

You created Grandma and
you created ladybugs.

Your creations are a wonder!

Glimpses...

June 1

Oooooops, God!

Look what day it is!

What a journey we've had as each day
in this year has been a new adventure.

As Grandma remembers that this is
still a year in progress, maybe today
could be the start of something new.

Like the freshness of a new year.

Awareness...

June 2

How much longer, God?

When will we get there?
How much longer do I have to endure?
Isn't it time yet?

Whatever Grandma's question is today,
may enlightenment be her blessing today.

Awakening...

June 3

I'm free, Lord!

I'm flying free!

Remember what Grandma felt like when
she went down a slide in the park?

Maybe she felt free like a soaring bird.

I hope Grandma still feels
that way sometimes.

Zooming...

June 4

Warm God,

How many nights does Grandma
tuck herself into bed at night?

Would you tuck her in as she lays
her head gently upon her pillow?

Settling in...

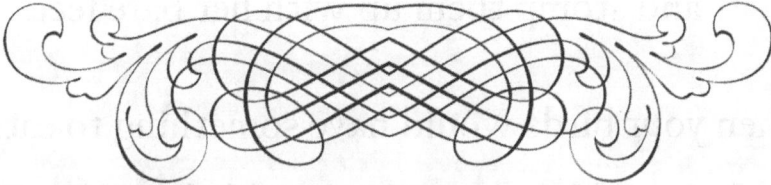

June 5

Help God!

Sometimes I am just fed up with my life.

It seems like such a struggle sometimes.

If Grandma ever feels that way, would
you shower her with kindness –
like you do for me?

Awaiting a sprinkle...

June 6

Whimsical Father,

Does Grandma have some crackers in her cupboard that are old and can't be eaten?

If she wants to, she could take the crackers outside and stomp them up with her bare feet.

Then your birds would have something to eat, and Grandma could do something ticklish and outrageous.

Plentifully...

June 7

Dear Jesus,

Sometimes I just try too hard.

Does Grandma ever try too hard?

Help us to relax and allow things to unfold when we're trying too hard.

Deep breath...

June 8

Dear God,

I can always trust Grandma to have an open heart when I see her.

I can always trust that Grandma cares about me.

I can always trust that you walk with Grandma through her life.

Trusting...

June 9

I surrender God!

I can't do this by myself.

What does Grandma need to surrender to you?

Help her hand it to you.

Offering...

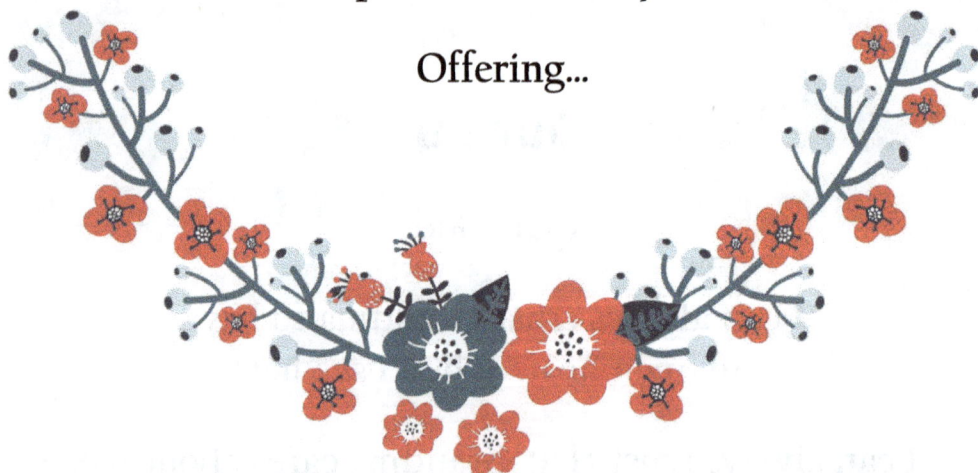

June 10

Can you hear her Jesus?

Grandma is singing.

There is a song in her heart.

Is it okay if she sings out loud?

She can hear her song when she sings out loud.

Rejoicing...

June 11

Just a minute Lord.

You know, this relationship I have with my
Grandma has taken time.

Each day it changes; every year we learn
new things that change our lives.

I'm grateful for the time I've had to share with Grandma,
for that time has made us who we are today.

I'm grateful for the time we have yet to experience.

Timing...

June 12

Hey God?

How does Grandma feel when she thinks of death;
her death or perhaps the death of a loved one?

I believe when someone dies you've given us a
time to cry,
to have joy,
to feel empty,
to feel fulfilled,
to miss someone,
to celebrate the life.

I don't understand it all! If Grandma needs some
understanding, I'd like it if you'd be there for her.

Puzzled...

June 13

Yippee Jesus!

Grandma won! We played a game and Grandma won.
I like it when Grandma wins. I hope she wins today.

Celebrate...

June 14

This is Yours, God.

Grandma is yours. Thank you for sharing her with me.

You made a good people when you made Grandma.

I'm glad she listens to you.

Sowing...

June 15

You there, Father God?

If Grandma is tired from carrying heavy burdens, help her come your way so that you can give her rest.

Humbly...

June 16

Star light, star bright,
first star I see tonight.

Shine on Grandma's face
and make her eyes sparkle.

She wished she may,
she wished she might.

Could Grandma have her wish tonight?

June 17

Christ Jesus,

Today I hugged a tree –
thanking the tree for all it does for me.

Maybe Grandma could hug her chair today.

Her chair does so much for her.

Supportingly...

June 18

Constant Lord,

Sometimes Grandma cries.

Would you wipe her tears and
let her know you're there with her?

Comfort...

June 19

Wake up God!

Wake up! Wake up! Did you see what Grandma did?

Isn't she amazing?! Grandma is a blessing!

Blooming...

June 20

Ahhhhh Father,

Shower Grandma with different peaces today.

(Here's an umbrella if you need one.)

June 21

Mighty One,

Can you catch sea monsters?

Today there is a sea monster in my life.

Could you help me tame the wild monster?

If Grandma needs help with a wild
monster, would you help her too?

Out of control...

✠

June 22

God,

Is Grandma ever discouraged?

When I'm discouraged, sometimes
Grandma knows just the right thing to say.

If I could say the right thing to her,
bless my lips for her.

Meaning...

June 23

Summer Son,

The sun is golden and warm. It feels good to go outside and feel your sunshine on my skin. When Grandma goes someplace today and she feel your warm sun on her Grandma self, maybe she'll think it's me reaching down to give her a hug.

Toasty warm...

June 24

Hi God.

You know Grandma gives of herself in so many ways.

She's been generous all her life as far as I can tell.

As much as she gives, I wonder if today she could receive.

I hope Grandma is aware of the many blessings she receives today.

Reciprocating...

June 25

Time for a pow-wow, God.

Grandma calls it 'council of wars'.

It's where the family gets together
and makes decisions about things.

Well, you're part of the family.

So Grandma and I have decided
to care about each other.

What do you think?

June 26

Good and gracious Lord,

Today I'd like to chat about meditating.

Meditating is a great way to learn, to listen.

Meditating with others creates community.

Meditating alone opens new places in my soul.

In my heart today, I'm
meditating with Grandma.

Soul searching...

June 27

Loving Father,

Today is hug awareness day.
I'm just going to declare it!

As Grandma journeys through her day, help her to be
aware of the many ways people hug her.

Help her be aware when she goes to church,
when I see her, when she gets to go out for ice cream.
Ice cream is a hug for our bellies.

Hugs and kisses...

June 28

How about it, God?

Playtime for Grandma.

When was the last time Grandma just had some play time?

Maybe playing house or playing the piano.

Maybe she could play a game of Yahtzee with a friend.

Frolicking...

June 29

Anointing Lord,

When Grandma takes a bath,
does she ever splash just for fun?

Does she ever drop a spoon in the sink
and enjoy a splash?

Maybe Grandma could have a good splash today.

Make it fun and cleansing.

Sprinkles...

June 30

Great teaching One,

Grandma has lots of books in her house.
Does she have any book friends?

You know, books that comfort,
or books that touch her soul.

The Bible is one of my book friends.

Help Grandma find the perfect book friend today.

Preparing...

July 1

Here God!

Grandma has a paper bag.

This is where she keeps things that are a crisis to her.

Here's Grandma's paper bag –
we're going to let you take care of these things for her.

Patiently...

July 2

Watchful God,

What is it like for you to watch us live our lives?

Sometimes I like to watch birds.
Flower watching is a beauty.
Thought watching can be enlightening.

What is Grandma watching today?

Observing...

July 3

Refreshing Savior,

There's nothing in the world quite like
a gentle summer shower.

It may not be raining today at Grandma's house.

The next time you give her a gentle summer sprinkle, let
her know it's okay to step outside
– without an umbrella
– without a rain bonnet.

She can pretend that I'm showering her
with hugs and kisses.

Freshen up...

July 4

God of our land,

Today is a day we recognize

our country's independence.

Surely Grandma feels

independent herself sometimes.

Thank you, Lord, for the integrity

that comes from being independent.

As a patriot...

July 5

Caring Lord,

Sometimes other people are unkind, and I feel betrayed.

Does Grandma ever feel betrayed?

When she has these feelings, I hope she remembers that you can help her with that.

Would you please help us understand?

Mending...

July 6

Wise One,

You know how it feels to stretch your arms and
legs after a good night of rest?

Waking up with a bit of sun peeking through the
curtains and stretching all my parts in an energizing
way to start my day and can be refreshing.

Maybe Grandma will take time to have
a good stretch today.

And when she does, could you fill her cells
with life and spunk?

Eagerly...

July 7

Hello God,

It's me.

I had a thought about prayers.

I think when we say prayers it's like a
fresh coat of paint for the soul.

You know, it keeps the soul in good working order.

Grandma must have a special prayer she'd
like to share with you today.

Calmly...

July 8

Great Navigator,

The time has come for the makings of an adventure. I think adventure finds people sometimes. Other times, I think we need to go looking for a bit of adventure.

Adventure comes in all shapes and sizes. Maybe Grandma is due for an adventure. Maybe a trip to the hamburger store or maybe a trip to a gift shop for some window shopping is the adventure in store.

Maybe her adventure could be having a chat with a friend.

Happening....

July 9

Tender Lord,

Is Grandma hiding something?

Is there something she just doesn't want to admit to?

You know, Lord, there are times when I just don't want to admit to things – like own up to my thoughts or actions.

When I can admit to things, it helps me to be honest with myself.

Even something simple like – I admit that I could be more patient with someone.

I hope Grandma can be honest with herself today.

Willingly...

July 10

Astounding Savior,

I made an invention once.

I was in the kitchen, and I invented a recipe.

I invented a prayer once.

I invented my life when I made a choice to be who I am.

What sort of things does Grandma invent?

Does she invent goodness?

She invents a great glass of lemonade.

What is Grandma going to invent today?

Building...

July 11

Good day God.

It's the beginning of a new day.

I'm going to begin playing the violin today.
What is Grandma beginning?

How does she begin her day when she
first opens her eyes in the morning?

How does she begin her visits with people –
what's in her mind and heart?

How does she begin her travel to the church?

Begin again...

July 12

Over here, Lord.

I want to try something.
I want to try something new today.

I'm going to try whispering something I like
about Grandma and set it free upon a breeze.

Do you think you could carry my sentiments
on that breeze all the way to her house?

Could you make it so she feels it in her heart?

Whoosh...

July 13

Wow God!

Today is someone's birthday.

What if it were my birthday today?

Do you know what my favorite birthday present is?

I'll tell you. It's the ability to love Grandma.

Thank you for allowing me to have a Grandma to love.

Reaching out...

July 14

Dear Father,

AAAAAAAAAAAAAAAAaaaaaaaaaaaaaaaaaaaa!

Can you hear me?

I'm shouting at the top of my lungs!
Did you hear me singing out loud in the car yesterday?

AAAAAAAAAaaaaaaaa!

It feels good to shout a little!

Does Grandma ever shout to herself?!

Quietly or out loud?

Do you think she could get in her car,
drive out to the farm, and let out a shout?

I LOVE YOU GRANDMA!

July 15

Hey God,

I meant to do that.

I intended to clean up the kitchen
and do the laundry.

I meant to do it, and I did it!
I just wonder what Grandma's
intentions are for today.

Whatever it is that she intends, I
wonder if you could be with her as she
accomplishes her intentions.

Intentionally...

July 16

Jesus, I want to ask you something.

It seems to me that there are gifts unknown in being unknown.

What are your thoughts?

Let's take Grandma for example.
She's relatively unknown – I mean she's known, but she's not known like say Abe Lincoln is known.

It seems to me that one of the gifts of being unknown is how a person might change the world.

I believe that the world is a better place because my Grandma takes the time in her life to let me be a part of her life.

Isn't that good for your world somehow?

Curiously...

July 17

Dear Lord,

Does Grandma ever have a hard time
getting her motor revved up?

Today when I was getting ready to go to
work, I wasn't quite as motivated
as I usually am.

If Grandma needs something to
help her get her motor going today,
I would especially appreciate it if
you'd help her out.

Varoom...

July 18

Blessed Savior,

You know my Grandma?
She's always seemed confident to me.

Is it possible that she ever has a day
when she doesn't feel so confident?

When I don't feel very confident, I
usually ask you for a dose of courage.

It's a fancy thing that you always
provide confidence for me when I ask
(sometimes even when I don't ask).

Maybe if Grandma wants some
confidence about something you
could give her a little boost.

Accomplishing...

July 19

Prrrrecious One,

You must know how wonderful it is to be a
cat that gets a good back rub.

My cat just purrrrrs when I give him a good rub.

I was thinking that maybe Grandma could
pretend that I'm there with her in her living room,
and I'm giving her a back rub.

Feel my warm hands as they nurture you?
(Think I can hear her purring!)

Ahhhhhhhh.

July 20

Ummm, God?

I see what you did. Along with summer shadows, I like
dancing with my shadow – we're always in step together!

Well, Grandma may not be dancing, but maybe
she could wave her arms or hands and
dance with her shadow today.

One, two, three. One, two, three...

July 21

Pssst! Jesus!

Here's an idea. You know how many
thoughts Grandma has.

She has lots of thoughts about so many things.
Wouldn't it be a pleasant surprise if she
would just write down one or two of her
thoughts on a piece of paper?

Then she could hide them, maybe in the
silverware drawer, coffee can, or in the
cupboard with her bath towels.

Then someday, she'll find her thoughts
and she can smile about them.

Autographs...

July 22

Whew, God!

That dream Grandma had last night!
She may or may not remember it!

Maybe she remembers a dream she has –
maybe not a night dream, but a daydream.
You know, like – I'd like to see children.

Bless her dream.

Take care of Grandma's dreams in the way
that is best for her.

Astonishingly...

July 23

Joyous Savior,

I wanted you to know that I enjoy my life.
What does Grandma enjoy?

Does she enjoy the nature around her?
Does she enjoy this day?
Does she enjoy her 'Cadillac walker'?
Does she enjoy spending time with Grandpa?
Does she enjoy herself?

In joy...

July 24

Powerful God,

Grandma is such a woman of strength.

Where did she find the strength to
transition Grandpa into a nursing home?

Where did that strength come from
when she moved from her familiar
house to an apartment?

Did you see her strength when Grandpa
got grumpy and yelled at her?

If she's looking for strength,
please provide her with
all that she needs.

Sturdy...

July 25

Lord Jesus,

You know what the Upper Room is?

Do we have upper rooms in our souls?

What do we keep in our upper rooms?

Is it the attic where we store stuff?

Is it an intimate place where we gather
with ourselves in your midst?

Is it a place where we go to when
we're looking for solace?

What is Grandma's upper room?

Pondering...

July 26

Poetic Father,

I noticed something about a particular word – Expressive.

Pull it apart a little and you have ex-press. If you ex-press

something, do you let it go or set it free?

What are some things that Grandma wants to express?

She expresses that she cares.

She expresses that she is concerned.

She expresses herself.

Allow her to express something from her heart.

Eloquently...

July 27

(To the tune of Lead On O King Eternal)

Lead on, Grandma, I'm watching.

You have a solid path.

Please let me walk beside you, as I enjoy your hand.

Remember that I love you, remember that I care!

Whenever you are lonely, remember God is there.

July 28

Father,

Grandma is a grandma because she's older than me.

Older means aging. Aging means what?

When Grandma ages, does she awaken the
part of herself that understands it's natural to age?

When aging happens does she accept
that she's an old person?

Old persons are blessings and I think Grandma is a fine one.

Walk with Grandma as she ages.   Maturing...

July 29

Courageous God,

When was the last time that Grandma tried something new?

Does she ever have a hankering to give something a try?

Would you give her a gentle nudge and let her know it's okay to try something new today?

Try doing something differently; try changing the order of your day.

Maybe try a food item you've never had before.

Try, try, try, try, try.

Guarding...

July 30

God,

There's a good book that I enjoy
reading in from time to time.
It's called Grandma.

It's a book that has many varied chapters.
The book happens because
Grandma lives her life.

When she starts her day,
she begins a new portion of the book.

This book has many tones and melodies.

If you read carefully, there are
goodies that appear between the lines.

I like the book called Grandma.

Absorbing...

July 31

It's party time, Jesus.

What are we celebrating?

I'll tell you what we're celebrating.

We're celebrating Grandma's house.

We're celebrating Grandma's life.

Let's celebrate Grandma's marriage and her
haircuts and her cookies.

Celebrate with Grandma –
whatever she wants to celebrate.

Praising...

August 1

Steady Savior,

What does Grandma believe in?

I believe in goodness and truth. I believe in you.
I believe in Grandma, she's one of your children, too.

I believe in myself. I believe in family.
I believe in writing and I believe in song.

I believe you're with her and Grandma believes you, too.

Faithfully...

August 2

God?

Tell me about suspicion.

Is Grandma ever suspicious?

What is she suspicious of?

Handle Grandma's suspicions with caring.

Journeying...

August 3

Hi Father.

One, two, three, four. One, two, three, four.
Faster now, then slower.

One, two, three. One two, three.
Softer. Now louder.

I was wondering about Grandma's tempo today.
What is her tempo?

Make it a tempo that helps her and make it just right.

Infinitely...

August 4

Wondrous One,

Let's visit about tenderness a little.
Boo-boos require tenderness, kitties require it, and
tenderness is for people, too.

I think Grandma needs tenderness on an occasional day or
two. Grandma is always tender with me and I desire to
share the same with her.

Help her to receive tenderness and be tender for herself
whenever it's meant to be.

Softly...

August 5

Yikes God!

It feels like it's time to be a little crazy.

Is it okay for Grandma to be a little crazy, too?

What would happen if Grandma ate ice cream with a fork?

How about putting a squeeze of a fresh
orange slice in her bath water?

Would it be okay for her to eat desert first today?

Could she wash her hands with milk
or sprinkle vanilla in her coffee?

Wild things...

August 6

Spiritual Father,

Remember years back when
Grandma and Grandpa married?

What a divine and holy institution –
this marriage.

There must be many lessons in
Grandma's life she learned by being married.

Thank you for teaching her –
thank you for helping Grandma learn.

Loving...

August 7

Dear God,

If Grandma could bend down on her knees
and make chalk drawing on the sidewalk,
what kind of pictures would she make?

Would she draw a hopscotch?
Would she draw people with smiling faces?

Imagining...

August 8

Jazzy Jesus,

I did the laundry today and you know what happened?
As I washed the clothes, I allowed you to wash my soul.

When I dried the clothes, I hung out
my soggy thoughts to dry.

While folding clothes, I found a place for
one of my cares and worries.

When I put my clothes away, I handed my heart to you.
(Grandma does laundry, too, you already know!)

Reverently...

August 9

Dear Lord,

Things, things, things, things.

Things are things.

People are people.

Family is family.

Life changes from the moment we are born.

One of the constant things in our lives is your love.
Another constant is that life will surely change every day.

Some days it changes more than others.

As Grandma goes through some of those bigger changes,
I appreciate knowing that you are there to guide her
through it, to help her accept what needs to be accepted,
to help her change what she can change, and to help her
perspectives to be aligned in their proper place.

Changing...

August 10

Great Navigator One,

We travel with our hearts, our cars, our souls, our minds, and our feet.

Which way do we go?

How do we decide where to go?

Sometimes it's hard for me to know the correct decision, or which decision is best for all involved.

I do know, though, that when I make a decision there is freedom in moving on.

Miraculously, the life that is supposed to happen as a result of the choice, happens and what golden opportunity is presented there.

Thank you.

August 11

Yodel-le-hee-hoo Lord!

I was thinking about giant things today.
You know I think my Grandma is a quiet giant.

She has a heart bigger than the state of Texas and she has a
soul that's deeper than the ocean.

She goes about her existence each day, taking on the
challenges that face her, and she just keeps on keeping on –
steady as she goes.

She is a quiet giant, and she blesses my life so richly.

Can she hear me?

August 12

There you are, God.

I see you dancing in the playful waves
in the swimming pool.

I see you dancing in the rush of people going
to the store to pick up groceries.

I see you dancing when Grandma plays the piano
without any music.

When was the last time Grandma danced?

Do you suppose she could, even now,
play some gentle music and dance a gentle dance?

I imagine that if she danced,
she would smile from the inside out!

Wheeeee!

August 13

God,

I know it must seem to you that I ask a lot of questions.

I ask questions because I'm curious,
because I want direction, because I want to
uncover the miracle of the moment.

Asking is something I sometimes forget to do though,
because I just want to take care of things on my own.

When Grandma needs or wants something from
someone, whether it's you or another friend,
would you help her to feel free to ask?

Exploring...

August 14

Once Upon a Time, God,

...there was a child that was born
and she had her whole life ahead of her.

She was unaware, then, of the wonderment that
she would shower on your world because
she was going to be my Grandma.

Now she is my Grandma, and has been
since the day I was born.

The story continues to unfold...

August 15

Hello, God?

It's hot out here today!
Thank you for warmth.

Now that it's known that today is a hot day, what can
Grandma do to cool down?

What will be refreshing? A splash of cool water on her face?
An air conditioner? A cool bath?
A blessing from you?

Whoooosh!

August 16

Uhm, Lord?

You know what I'm hungry for?

I'd really like a root beer float – ice cream and root beer – mmmm. Just sounds really good.

What's Grandma hungry for today?

It's my desire that whatever it is that Grandma's hunger is, you could present an opportunity for her to quench her hunger.

Satisfying...

August 17

Dear Grandma,

This is God. How are you today?

Why don't you draw a picture today.
You have pens and pencils and a spot of paper.

Use lots of colors, use only one color.

Draw a picture that reminds you of something that comforted you as a child.

Remember you are still a child sometimes.

Thank you for drawing...

August 18

But God,

I just don't feel like doing that today. I'd rather just avoid dealing with that mess right now. Thank you for allowing me to avoid things; thank you for allowing me to learn from the 'void'.

What is Grandma avoiding?
Can you help her with that, please?

Face to face...

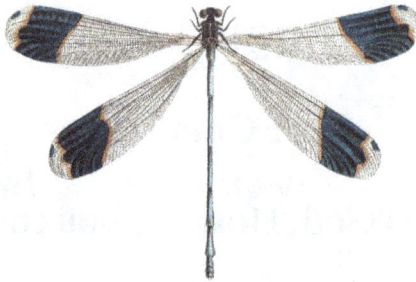

August 19

Yes Lord Jesus?

... I see...

August 20

Happy Father,

It's been a long time since Christmas.

I'm feeling like I'd like to give my Grandma a gift today.

I was wondering if you could stir a memory in my
Grandma's heart and let the memory
be a gift for her soul.

Stir a memory that's just right for her today.
Maybe a memory about something funny she heard
her Daddy or Mommy say.

Astonishingly...

August 21

Oh, Wise One,

You inspire me. Grandma inspires me.
What inspires Grandma?

What stirs her up?

What happens when she is
inspired by another person?

What sparks her imagination?
What's inspiring Grandma today?

Intriguingly...

August 22

Loving Father,

Today I just want to love.
I want to love that person that is rude to me at the store.

I want to love that person that speaks
disrespectfully toward me.

I want to love the way my life is.
I want to love the special gift my Grandma shared with me.

I want to love.

Loving...

August 23

Well God,

I want to do something for fun today.

I made some jello just because I wanted to play with it.
I made green jello.

It wiggles when I touch it.
It feels funny when I squish it between my fingers.

Isn't it silly when I try to eat jello with my hands?
It's fun to use a big serving spoon and get a great big bite.

What would happen if Grandma played with jello?
Did she ever play with jello?

Would it be okay for her to play with jello?

Outrageously...

August 24

Look here God!

Thank you for what you showed me today.

What does Grandma see?
What does she visualize her ideal day to be?

When she thinks of the coming autumn,
what does she see?

Sensing...

August 25

Ha ha ha Father.

I can't seem to stop laughing!

This just started being a little chuckle,
then it turned into a giggle.

From there I lost control and now I'm laughing
so hard I have tears in my ears!

Heeee heeee ha ha, heeeee, heeee!

Grinning...

August 26

Okay God!

Today I was drawing a picture on my driveway.

I used some of those big pieces of chalk
and drew faces and butterflies.

With the yellow one, I drew a big sunshine
and with the red one I made birds.

Did Grandma ever play with chalk?

Or was chalk only used in the classroom during school?
Does Grandma have a chalk story?

If Grandma had chalk,
what would she draw on the sidewalk?

Originally...

August 27

Yummy God,

One of my favorite summer foods is grapes.

Does Grandma have any grapes?

How many grapes can she put in her mouth at once?

I think I can get 13 grapes in my mouth.

Sometimes I put too many in my mouth and
grape juice squirts out on the table.

Now that Grandma lives by herself,
you think she might try playing with grapes?

Frivolous...

August 28

Dear Lord,

In Grandma's house there is a little box. In the little box there are some wishes.

These are Grandma's personal wishes that she has for herself and other people.

Could you ignite one of those wishes so that life happens in a good way for Grandma?

Patiently...

August 29

Wait God!

Give me some time to work on this. I just need a little time.

Time can be so healing. What time is it for Grandma?

If she needs time, would you grant it to her?

If it's time to get moving, will you nudge her in the right direction?

Tick tock...

August 30

Lord,

I was wondering about something.
As we go through our lives, we have
dreams that we wish for –
dreams that we want to come true.

I know Grandma has dreams, too.
Do we ever get to the end of those dreams?

It seems to me that when we attain a goal
or reach 'those points' in our lives that
the dreams then change and
we just keep on striving.

How does that work?

Curious...

August 31

Amazing Father,

This is the last day of this month.

There won't be any more days in
August this year.

Make today something special
for Grandma.

Open her heart so she
can discover what is so special
about this day.

Gratefully...

September 1

Bravo Dear Savior!

Grandma must be clapping her hands.
I hear that thunderous applause.

Is she clapping because she's singing a song
and keeping time? Is she clapping because she
appreciates something someone has done?

Is she clapping because she wants to hear that sound?
Is she clapping just because she feels like doing it?

Embracing...

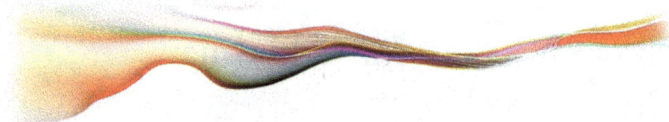

September 2

Caring Lord,

I know there are people who live in the clouds and watch
over me.

Who lives in the clouds and watches over Grandma?

I hope she is aware of her cloud friends today and
that she says thank you for all they are for her.

Tremendously...

September 3

Articulate Father,

You speak to us in so many varying languages.
Some of them we understand and others we don't.

Grandma is the same way.

She speaks lots of languages too –
English, heart, coffee, candy, hugs,
helps, dinners, cards, letters, prayers.

Help Grandma to speak in the way that is best
for each situation today.

Glowing...

September 4

Working Father,

You are always available to us, any
moment of any day or night.

For the fruits we enjoy because of
your labors we give you thanks.

Help Grandma to know that I'm
thankful, too, to know that her
love is always there for me.

Surely...

September 5

Faithful Savior,

My Grandma is one of your faithful servants.

She helps me live life.
She prays for me and she loves me
with her heart of gold.

She asks for your guidance and
she reads about you.

I just want to say thank you
for being faithful to her.

Contentedly...

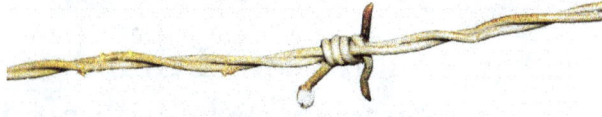

September 6

Dear God,

Nothing is right today.
Nothing is working right.

Everything I try to do just doesn't work out
the way I'm intending for it to.

I doesn't feel good, and life is just hard today.

Does Grandma ever feel this way?
I think she does, because she is one of your children.

If something isn't right for Grandma,
help her through that.

Help her embrace what is hard and help her learn.

Seeking...

September 7

What do you think, Lord?
What are your impressions of Grandma?

My impression of Grandma is that
sometimes she feels afraid.

I think she feels great to be alive sometimes.

Sometimes Grandma feels like
peanut brittle and other times she
feels like a cuddly teddy bear.

Impressions...

September 8

Enthusiastic Spirit,

Let's play a game. It's called a random game.

Grandma and I are going to take a book and allow
the book to open to the page it wants to open to.

Then we're going to read a bit from the book and
let the book touch our lives in some way today.

Boldly...

September 9

It's so good to be home, God.

You know when you're away on a trip and you come
home, you know how good your own bed feels
when you crawl in for that first night's sleep?

The bed feels like an old friend and the way your
house smells just makes your senses know
that you're home, really home.

I'd like it if Grandma could feel that feeling today and
that she could feel really good about being where she is.

Be calmed...

September 10

Fabulous Father,

When was the last time
Grandma made a new friend?

I like that feeling of making a new
friend. It's like my person-tree
gets bigger and has more flowery,
leafy blooms on it.

Sometimes old friends become like
new friends when I discover
new things about them.

I hope Grandma still
makes new friends.

Superbly...

September 11

Wispy God,

A wonderful breeze you did create this morning. It's

like a hint of autumn that is about to befall.

It's refreshing when you give us little

hints of the changing seasons.

It's kind of like a lesson to apply to ourselves

as our life-seasons change.

I'm thanking you for all of your seasons

and the way you introduce them –

nature seasons and natural life seasons.

Serendipitously...

September 12

Wondrous and Wise Creator,

Let's chat about this concept of things that last forever.

Lives don't last forever, but your care and guidance does.

People in their human form don't last forever,
but your love does.

Grandma is important to me.
I know that one day she will not be here.
Won't the spirit of her last forever?

As long as I choose to keep it alive?
I believe Grandma will always be with me –
in one way or another.

Salubriously...

September 13

Great God,

The world feels different when
the people in it are back into
the routine of school.

The whole heartbeat of the world
feels different to me.

Has Grandma ever noticed that?
What's it like for her when
it's school-time again?

Inquisitively...

September 14

Truth or Dare?

Dare ya!
I dare you, Grandma,
to let me love you more.

I dare ya! Dare ya, dare ya!

Leaping...

September 15

Just for fun, God.

Let's have a piece of cake with Grandma today.

I don't know if she is going to have any cake today –
maybe she can have some pretend cake or something.

Here we go.
We'll sit down right here at the table and have some cake.

I'm going to eat my cake with my fingers,
so I can lick off the icing when I'm finished.

How's Grandma going to have her cake today?

Wild and free...

September 16

Nurturing Savior,

How are Grandma's eyes today?

Do they feel rested?

Do they feel tired or scratchy?

Are they sparkling with spunk
and get-up-and-go?

Whatever the way of Grandma's
eyes today, thank you for her eyes.

I'm glad she can see.

Luminously...

September 17

All right then, God.

Music time. Grandma is full of music – she listens,
she creates, she allows music to move her soul.

When Grandma feels like it, could you talk with her about
personal things while she listens to music?

She can pick out something that she likes to listen to, turn
it on, lay down or sit comfortably in her chair.

Then she can close her eyes and let the music open the
doors in her soul.

Then you can touch her heart in just the perfect way.

Treasure hunting...

September 18

Hey God,

You know how we are always welcoming newborn babies into our world?

I'm thinking that we need to welcome old born babies too – old born babies like grandmas and grandpas.

Grandma, you are deeply wanted.
Grandma, welcome to our world.
Grandma, thank you for being here.

Pampering...

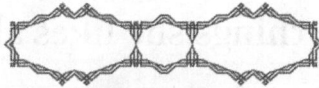

September 19

Dear Holy Spirit,

There are days when Grandma seeks solitude.
Solitude is good for us now and then.

It's okay to ask for it and it's okay to create it.

When Grandma seeks solitude, provide her with exactly what she's looking for.

Deep breath...

September 20

Gracious Father,

Did Grandma ever write a letter to herself and send it?

I wonder if she would be willing to give herself such a gift.

She could write herself a love letter and write
about all the things she likes about herself.

She could even say "I love you" to herself.

She could write a memory letter and
write down some memory gifts to rediscover
when her package comes in the mail.

Insightfully...

September 21

Embracing Father,

I'm wondering about something.

I'm wondering if it would be okay for Grandma to bang on pots and pans.

She could make her own little drum set; use different spoons and different dishes.

She doesn't have to bang loud, unless of course she wants to.

What would it feel like if Grandma really banged on pots and pans?

What would it be like if I could see her?

Energetically...

September 22

Everlasting Spirit,

I read a chapter of one of my favorite
books out loud today.

I picked up that book, sat down in my chair,
and read to myself.

I learn different things when I read out loud to myself.

Maybe Grandma could read out loud to herself some day.

Whether it's a book, a letter, or
maybe the words to a favorite song.

Pioneering...

September 23

(Another song, to the tune of Three Blind Mice)

Grandma cares.
She is fair.
See how she loves? O how she loves!

She goes to bed and she rests her head.

She loves her husband and is a good wife.
She plays the piano and smells real nice.

Grandma sneezed. A tissue please!

September 24

Guess what, God?

Grandma is wearing two different shoes today.
A house shoe and a dress shoe.

Or, maybe it was two regular shoes but they
were different colors.

Well, okay.
I don't really know if she's wearing two different shoes –
I suspect, though, that she's at least wearing
a left shoe and a right one.

Bless Grandma's shoes!

September 25

God of Man,

What is Grandma's quest in life?

I'm sure her quest is different today than
it was ten or even five years ago.

As she seeks her own purpose and life quest,
I thank you for illuminating Grandma's way to discovery.

Envisioning...

September 26

Master Adventurer,

I took myself for a walk in the woods today.
I enjoy the wonders of the earth when I
walk amongst your creations.
It's a good time for my heart and soul to re-align.

Does Grandma remember walking through
the woods or in the mountains?

What sort of things did she discover in these times?

Maybe the woods Grandma experienced in her
life have nothing to do with trees.

Walking...

September 27

Holy God,

Grandma and I grew up in different times.

I find it amazing that we can share so many common threads in our lives – even given the differences in lifetimes.

I'm grateful that my heart is open to having Grandma in it. She has her own place there.

Someday I will draw a picture of her place in my heart.

I'll have to invent colors required to represent her spot.

Smashingly...

September 28

Radiant Father,

I like it when the sun shines on Grandma as she makes her journey from place to place.

Did you notice the wondrous thing that happens when she stands in the sun just right?

Have you absorbed the wonder of her silhouettes?

I like to imagine, even when I am not with her, that Grandma's silhouette walks with me.

Casting...

September 29

Splendid God,

I like your autumn colors. Gold, flaming reds and oranges, brilliant yellows and soft browns.

I was thinking that Grandma might find a beautiful autumn leaf and bring it into her home today.

If I were there, I'd get one for her.

Shades of your world...

September 30

Hey God,

Can we talk about something a little unusual?

Now that I'm married and enjoy the sanctity of sharing
life with my companion, I'm curious about something.

Grandma and Grandpa surely must have been lovers.

I've never really thought about my
Grandparents as lovers, but surely, they are.

What profound expressions we have in
sharing our lives as husband and wife.

Grandma and Grandpa surely must experience profound
depth in their sharing.

Special for them...

October 1

Oh Dear God,

Sometimes it is difficult for me to let go of
things past and get on with the here and now.

I learned a great way to let go and let you
create the peace that is ready to settle.

I write down my secret and I throw it away, or
I take my secret to you in communion and let you
handle it in the mastery that is uniquely yours.

I don't know if Grandma has anything that she'd like to
set free, but if she does, let her know of your presence.

Releasing...

October 2

Father God,

When you look into Grandma's eyes,
what do you see?

Have you seen the sparking
twinkle that never dims?

I'm pretty sure that's her guiding light.

Have you noticed the enriching blue
and purple that surrounds her?

Are those colors in your rainbows?

I like how Grandma feels down in her soul.

It's like a glowing radiation that
embraces and guides.

Splendor...

October 3

I Saw That, God!

I saw that when you made the leaves dance
in the autumn breeze.

I saw that when you made that leaf a graceful ballerina
as it let go of the branch it has clung to all summer.

I saw that when you cooled the warm
summer air to a brisk autumn air.

I saw that when you wrapped your arms
around Grandma's life and held her.

Peeking...

October 4

Wake Up Lord!

It's time to Whee!
Wheeeeeeee, wheeeeeee, wheee, wheeeeeeeeeeeee!

Grandma could use a good whee, too.
She can do it wherever she likes – her car, her bathtub, her
kitchen – just help her let out a good wheeeee!

Once again with feeling! With gusto!
Wheeeeeeeee!

Whirling...

October 5

God of Grace,

Thanks for letting us make mistakes.
I admit that I don't like it when I do mistakes,
but I also find it's such a good way to learn.

I'm sure there have only been a few, but when
Grandma does a mistake, I hope you're there to
teach just the right lessons.

Grace-Full...

October 6

Plentiful Savior,

Is there going to be enough?
Does Grandma have enough?

Will there be enough for Grandma?

Thank you for always supplying what is needed.

I hope Grandma has enough for today and all
the coming days.

Abundantly...

October 7

Stable and Steady Father,

Does Grandma ever experience stillness?

I mean the kind of stillness that happens
during the day – not during rest.

You know that kind of stillness that stops
the hustle and bustle of the day.

Mind, heart and body come together
and there is stillness.

You bless us richly when we are still.

Bless Grandma's stillness.

Tranquilly...

October 8

Over here, God!

I got in trouble today.
I felt like a child who'd been sent to go sit in the corner.

Does Grandma ever feel that way?
I guess we have that feeling because it's time
to be aware of something important.

If Grandma feels 'sent to the corner' grant
her the awareness of what is important.

Troubled...

October 9

God! God! God!

Congratulations are in order!
She did it! Grandma did it!

I don't know specifically know what she's
accomplished, but she's accomplished something.

Did you give her a "Job Well Done?"

Did you pat her on the back?
Did you tell her she's wonderful?

Ecstatically...

October 10

Super Duper Father,

Grandma and I are doing something fun today
and you're invited to play with us.

Take a small glass or cup and put a pen or pencil in it.
Then put a tissue over the pencil.

If you use your imagination it looks like an angel!

Now, every time you see your creation,
be aware that angels are among us and
thank them for playing with us.

Great game, huh?

Playing...

October 11

Fantastic Father,

Today I read a book and tears fell upon my face.

Sometimes I watch television and
I let tears sprinkle my lap or pillow.

These are good growing tears.

When Grandma feels like crying, I hope she will.

Strengthening...

October 12

Jumpin' Junipers, Jesus!

What's the big rush! Hurry, hurry, hurry.

Seems like there's just not enough hours
in the day to get it all done.

When Grandma feels rushed, I wonder if you could
help her realize what's most important and help her
let the rest of it go until another day.

Exhaling...

October 13

Father,

Thank you for hamburgers.
Sometimes hamburgers are just
what Grandma's tummy wants.
Mmmmmm. Her little taste buds
are happy when they wake up to
that burger taste – juicy pickles,
lettuce, a fresh tomato, a splash of
mustard and maybe a creamy
piece of cheese.
Think I'll have a burger, too!

Tasting...

October 14

God, alive and active,

Where is Grandma roaming today?

Where will her feet traverse?

Wherever she might be, whatever
she might be doing, maybe she will
just have a good ol' day today.

Presently...

October 15

Hear this prayer, Oh Lord.

Understanding is something that's difficult to find
occasionally. Is Grandma looking for understanding?

Does she want to be understood?
Or is she looking to understand someone else?

I found some understanding in my kitchen cabinet today.

Would you see that Grandma gets as
much of it as she needs?

Sharing...

October 16

Constant Spirit,

Do you ever take vacations?

Sometimes I take mini vacations in my mind,
without ever getting in the car to go somewhere.

Sometimes I really go someplace
and enjoy a vacation.

I've had some wonderful vacations with my
Grandma, in the mountains, on the farm,
camping, celebrating Thanksgiving – many
different vacations.

Thank you for the vacations,
Grandma remembers – thank you for the
vacation times she has within her mind.

Invigorating...

October 17

Hey God,

Does Grandma have any of that yummy
hot chocolate that she makes?

I'd like to be with her in her living room,
sipping on a mug of hot chocolate.

Would it be okay for Grandma to have a cup of hot
chocolate and pretend that I'm there with her?

We're talking about what's going on in our lives –
how people are and what's happening.

Fellowship...

October 18

Help! Jesus! Help!

I can be sooooo hard on my self sometimes.

Save me from myself! Help me!

Sometimes Grandma is hard on herself, too and could use a hand.

Would you lend her a hand when she's being hard on herself?

Asking...

October 19

Watchful Father,

Today I'm wearing a necklace that my Grandma gave me for a birthday many years ago.

I like wearing this necklace. When I wear it, it's like spending the day with my Grandma – I am aware of her presence in my life.

Let Grandma know that she's being thought about today.

Attentively...

October 20

Almighty God,

Do you suppose Grandma ever has a
hard time falling asleep at night?

Sometimes my mind is buzzing
around so ferociously that sleep
is a challenge to acquire.

When Grandma has a night that
finds her restless - bring her solace
so that rest finds her.

Patiently...

October 21

Knock, knock, God.

It's me.

This afternoon I took the time to relax –
simply for the sake of relaxing.

When I take time to relax, I like to imagine a
beautiful butterfly gently flying around me.

As the butterfly slowly moves from my head to my
toes, I imagine that she's sprinkling beautiful
powdery, sparkling dust on me that allows
my muscles to relax and rest.

I'd like to share my butterfly with Grandma,
if she'd invite her to come by for a spell.

Beautifully...

October 22

Smiling Father,

Thank you for teaching Grandma how to love.

Countless days in my life she has touched
my life in ways that only she can touch.

I wanted to let you know that
Grandma's exceptionally good at loving.

Receiving...

October 23

Hey you, God Being,

I found myself at the store today and I
bought myself a flower.

I put it on the table,
where all the activity happens.

When I see it, I think about Grandma,
and how she enjoys this type of
lovely creation you made.

This flower is for Grandma;
would you see that she gets it.

Pondering...

October 24

Extraordinary Lord,

Does Grandma ever get the blahs?
What are blah days for?

What are you trying to tell us?

If Grandma has a blah day, enlighten her path
so that she can be peaceful with her blahs.

Ho, humming...

October 25

Oh my, Lord.

Does Grandma ever eat too much?

Does she ever get that 'stuffed'
feeling after a big meal?

If Grandma finds herself feeling stuffed, I can
hear her being thankful for the opportunity
to be well fed.

Rejoicing...

October 26

Dear Father,

Thank you for medicine.
Grandma is at a point in her life
where she requires medicine to
help her body to be hospitable.

I'm grateful that she is able
to get what she needs, and
that we have medicine to
help us out as required.

Constantly...

October 27

God,

I'm having a bad hair day.

Not only is my hair uncooperative, but it seems like nothing is going the way it's supposed to today.

I suspect that Grandma happens upon a bad hair day now and then.

When she's having one of those days, could you share with her some of that patience that you shared with me?

Relentlessly...

October 28

Blessed Father,

Grandma has some bills to pay.

Sometimes it seems that there's more month than
a body's going to have money for.

You have always provided for Grandma, though.

She has always found a way to manage
through the rough places.

Thank you for being with her
through those times.

Tolerantly...

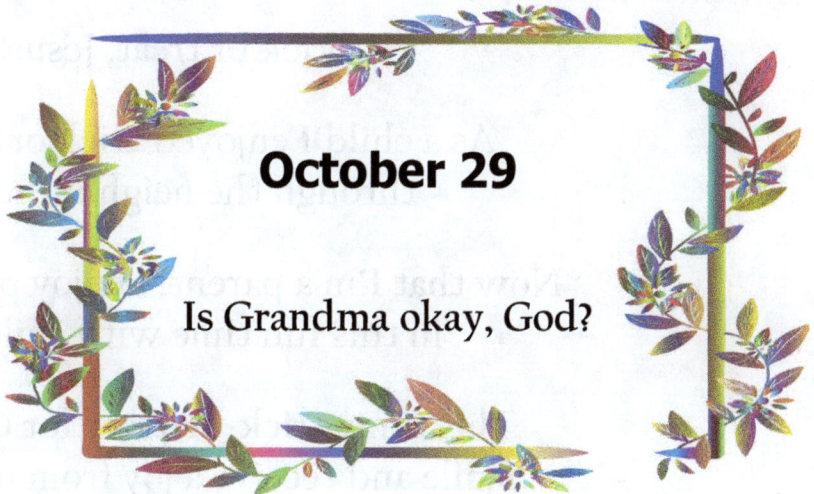

October 29

Is Grandma okay, God?

October 30

What if, God?

Suppose Grandma deliberately wore two different colored socks today?

If she's at home and no one is there to see, what would happen if she wore two different socks?

Maybe she'll give it a try and tell me what it was like.

Adventuring...

October 31

Trick or treat, Jesus!

As a child I enjoyed trick or treating through the neighborhood.

Now that I'm a parent, I enjoy participating in this fun time with children.

This is my trick-or-treat for Grandma. Smile and receive a joy from me to you.

Boo!

November 1

God,

Did she remember? Did Grandma remember what you reminded her about today? Reminders are invitations. Thank you for reminder blessings.

Recalling...

November 2

Holy Father,

Grandma gets a little cough now and then, especially during the cold months.

I know she keeps candy corn around the house, because I always snitch a piece when I go to visit her.

Grandpa always said that candy corn cured his cough.

Suppose it might help Grandma, too?

Nurturing...

November 3

Now and then, God,

In Grandma's closet there is a chest of drawers.
In those drawers there are many special things.

If she were to look in one of those drawers today,
I wonder if you would point out a special something
that would be a blessing for her today.

Surprises lurking...

November 4

Well God,

I spent some time just thinking about the
many ways that I love my Grandma.

Then I thought about an old friend
that I haven't seen for a while.

While I thought about this friend, I set some good
thoughts into flight to find the way to my friend's heart.

You bless us with the gift of having
old friends to think about.

Bless Grandma's friends.

Relationships...

November 5

Dear God,

I've got the munchies and I'd like to have a snack.

Let's have a snack with Grandma.
I'll cut up an apple and get out a jar of honey.

Now, Grandma first.
Take an apple slice, dip it in the honey and say
thank you for something you're grateful for.

My turn.
I'm thankful for warm clothes.

Okay, Grandma, your turn.

Delightfully...

November 6

Fostering Father,

I know that Grandma's Mommy has been
in your care for many years.

Does Grandma ever miss talking with her mother?

Would it be okay for her to write a letter to her mother?

Would it be okay for her to write a letter to
her Mom and maybe put it in a special place
so she can find it on another day?

Will Grandma's Mommy hear her thoughts and prayers?

Connecting...

November 7

Capable God,

This load that I'm carrying is too heavy.
Can you help me with this today?

What is Grandma carrying that is
keeping her from enjoying her day today?

Can you take that off her hands
and free her up a bit?

Tasking...

November 8

Enriching Lord,

What's Grandma doing today?
Are you with her?

Is Grandma completing
something today?

Did you give her some praise today?

Companions...

November 9

Amazing Father,

Grandmas are just miraculous.

They are different than moms and they are different than siblings.

Grandmas are important.

There are things only a Grandma can do and things only a Grandma can say.

Grandmas are irreplaceable yet required.

Grandmas are truly miraculous.

Astounded...

November 10

Delightful Spirit,

Thank you for the private little tickle that Grandma is going to have today.

I don't know what her tickle is going to be about – that's between you and Grandma.

I hope she'll enjoy her little tickles – maybe her insides will wiggle when she gets her tickle.

Cheerfully...

November 11

Beauteous One,

You know how much Grandma loves the moon.

If there is a moon for her to see this day or night, make it especially glorious for her.

Grandma tells me that God is in the moon.

You must be there to light our way in our darkest hours.

November 12

Knowledgeable Father,

You are surely wise in the way that
you design families to work.

Grandma raised her children well,
and then when it was time to set them
free to be people in this world of yours,
she let them go – and now look what has happened.

Now her kids have children of their own,
and they've let them go out into the world.

Now I can nurture my Grandma.

Splendor...

November 13

Reverent Father,

Are you with Grandma when she feels unmotivated?

Are you there to help light a fire in her spirit so that when the un-motivation is over, then she's ready to hit the ground running?

Shaking things up...

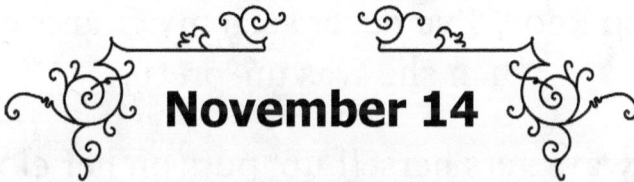

November 14

Tender Christ,

Today I'm remembering what it was like to sit in Grandma's lap as she held me and gently rocked in her chair. That is soothing to me. When Grandma needs some soothing, could you hold her in your mighty lap and rock her gently?

Sighing...

November 15

Heavenly Father,

You know I've never seen my Grandma
when she was un-pretty.

She always gets herself up, puts on her clothes,
makes up her face, and she's always
ready for the world.

She even goes to get her hair fixed.
She's always pretty.

Thank you for the many ways you help her
to be 'ready' for the world.

Preparing...

November 16

Subtle Spirit,

What a stunning experience – the prism.

Your light shines through and
makes all those lustrous colors.

Grandma is much like your prism!

Your light shines through her and a myriad
of other colors come blasting through!

Iridescence...

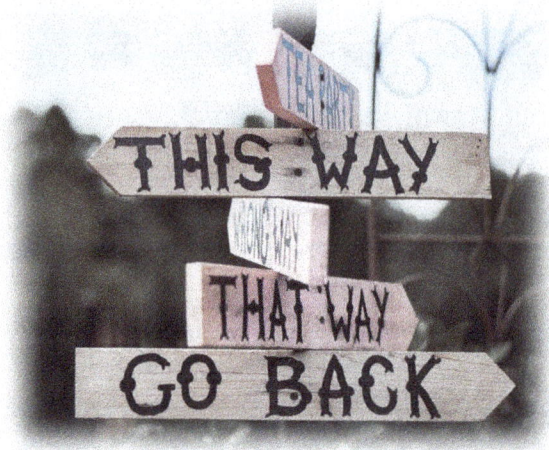

November 17

Durable God,

You know we've created these traffic sign thingies.

One for stop, one for go – all kinds of signs.

I think you must have given us this idea because when I see these signs, they are like signposts from you.

Maybe it's time for me to be cautious.

Maybe it's time for me to get on with it and go!

I hope Grandma is aware of your signposts today.

What will her direction be?

Fervently...

November 18

I'm curious, God,

What does Grandma see when she looks in the mirror?
What are the different faces that she sees?
Are the faces she observes the same
faces other people see?

What is it that other people see?
At times, Grandma is a good mirror herself.
When I see Grandma, I see pieces of myself.

Reflections...

November 19

Gracious Father,

You are one of the most patient beings!

Grandma has been molding herself
from the time she was born.

Look at what you guys have made!

How generous for you to allow us to be an active
part of creating our own outcomes in life.

Artistically...

November 20

Oh, Holy Spirit,

What a mighty breeze you're blowing today!
And it feels oh, so cold! Burrrrrrrr!

Wherever she is today, Holy One,
be sure she is safe and warm.

Be sure Grandma is safe and protected
from the chill.

Warm thoughts...

November 21

Wonderful Christ,

I pray today that Grandma's day is
filled with unexpected kindnesses.

Kind acts from different people, kind
blessing from you – like the sun,
or any gentle kindness that helps
Grandma's day to be full of blessings.

Gently...

November 22

Revealing Savior,

You always answer our prayers
in one way or another.

Just want to take a moment and say
thank you for doing that.

Thank you for responding to the prayers
my Grandma prays to you.

Thank you for responding to the
prayers I have for Grandma.

Attentively...

November 23

Guardian Lord,

Does Grandma ever feel lost?

You must always be with her,
because she always seems to find her way.

No, it might not be the way she thought she would go,
but you always manage to get her back on track.

Thank you for helping Grandma to find her way.

Roving...

November 24

Vast and Powerful God,

Congratulations! Grandma did it!

She's accomplished something
and I want to celebrate that.

Maybe she's accomplished
something deeply personal or
something she wanted to
accomplish for a friend.

She did it!

Congratulations on your
accomplishments Grandma!

Celebrating...

November 25

Amazing Father,

You gift us each day with the gift of a day.

You give this gift freely, as you allow us to make our days what we want them to be.

I hope that Grandma's day is perceived as a gift today.

That she awakens and has this day to live is a gift.

Hope she makes the most of it.

Choosing...

November 26

Bountiful God,

This is a day we give thanks for life,
thanks for love,
thanks for food,
thanks for home,
thanks for safety and grace.

I'm thankful for my Grandma – who she is,
what she is, and what that means to me.

Joyously...

November 27

Everlasting Father,

You've given us these senses – our eyes, ears, touch, taste and smell.

Another of your awesome senses is the senses that come with the heart – joy, sadness, angry, healthy, excitement, love.

These senses are all blessings you've given us so that our life is rich and real somehow.

Maybe Grandma will be aware of her senses today.

Mindfully...

November 28

Discovering One,

I was going through some of my family treasures and I found something my Grandma gave me.

I held it in my hand and close to my heart.

I felt her heart close to mine as I remembered the experiences associated with this treasure.

What treasure will Grandma uncover today?

Cherishing...

November 29

Loving Father,

You know how unselfish it is when a cat finds a lap to lay in?

It seems these creatures just come and share themselves.

And it is a wonderment that they tend to know just when their presence brings comfort and when their presence is meant to provide companionship.

Grandma is like that for me.

Would you help her realize how amazingly unselfish she is?

Graciously...

November 30

Hey God,

Is Grandma's mailbox happy?

Does her mailbox still get special packages?

Letters are like special private parties.

I hope Grandma still receives special
private parties in the mail!

Sending forth...

December 1

Hey Holy One,

It's the advent of something wondrous.

I saw Grandma light that candle and
I watched her eyes look deeply into the flame.

I'm not sure what she's seeing, but it
feels good to my insides.

Bless her as she experiences something wondrous today.

Anticipating...

December 2

Glorious Lord,

It's the last of the months we're going to have in this year.
Whatever this month is holding for Grandma,
I hope your loving guidance is there with her.

I know that some things will seem the same to her –
like other Decembers she's lived.

I also know that there are new things that will make
this December unlike any other she's had before.

Inspirationally...

December 3

Thank you Father.

Thank you for happy food.
Cranberry bread is happy food.

It has a subtle sweetness and a refreshing
zing all at the same time.

What is Grandma's happy food?

Would it be okay for her to have some?
Just a bit anyway?

Happy food not only tastes good,
but it nourishes the soul.

Scrumptiously...

December 4

Ring, ring. Ring, ring, God.

There is a bell in Grandma's house that has
deep meaning for her.

Well, when was the last time she heard that bell ring?

Maybe she could pick it up and ring that bell today.

Bless her memories and bless the sound that
fills her home and her heart.

Exuberantly...

December 5

Healing Father,

I'm not feeling too good today.

When I took my medicine,
I put a spoonful of sugar with it.

I got that idea from Grandma, you know.
I don't know which thing made me feel better,
the sugar or the medicine.

Anyway, it doesn't matter;
the main thing is I'm better now.

Mending...

December 6

God,

Does Grandma ever take a day off?

Is there ever a day when Grandma
can just wear her pajamas all
day long if she wants to?

Is there a day when she can go
without any make up?

Is there a day when she can be a
couch potato if she wants to be?

Bursting...

December 7

Great Father,

I have a tradition that I celebrate today.

It's a tradition called giving something or
doing something for someone else.

Grandma has that same tradition.
I learned it from her, you know.

Consecrate her tradition as she
exercises it today.

As always...

December 8

God,

You know how commercial the holidays can seem?

I think it's rather ironic that we as a world
have put so much emphasis on the
magical time that you've created for us.

Though people get caught up on the commercial
nature of this time, there's a part of me that giggles
inside because even in the hustle and fury, in some
way,
these beings are aware of your presence in their lives.

Observing...

December 9

Magical Savior,

Grandma loves pretty lights during the holidays.
Is there a special light that she can turn on in her house?

When she turns it on, I hope she smiles
and feels warm inside.

The moment her light comes on,
would you be so kind as to ignite
a special Grandma blessing?

Revealing...

December 10

God of Love,

Grandma made this blanket for me.

Does she have any idea how wonderful these naps
are, underneath her hand-made blanket?

For me it's like I'm in her lap resting
and she is holding me in her arms.

This is really special warmth.

Thank you, Grandma!

December 11

Father,

You know we have these staple things.
We use them to keep different pieces of paper together.

Did you make special kind of staples
that you use for families?

You know, Grandma and I are different,
but you somehow keep us together.

Bonding...

December 12

Watchful One,

What makes Grandma feel safe?

Are there special things she does to feel safe?

I know you are there to help her feel safe.

Bless Grandma's life so she feels safe.

Security...

December 13

Dear God,

You must have an amazing Christmas tree.

If each of your creations is a unique ornament,
I can just imagine what your tree looks like.

I see that Grandma ornament over there –
it looks just like my Grandma and oh so beautiful.

Decoratively...

December 14

Delightful Spirit,

I'm wondering about something.

If the little girl that turned into my Grandma had something she wanted to share with the woman that is now my Grandma, what would she want to share?

Can you help Grandma hear the little girl inside of her?

Introspectively...

December 15

Hello, God?

When Grandma puts on her gloves today, I hope she feels like you're there holding her hand.

Hands are good for holding. I'm holding Grandma's hands today.

I'm holding on to her dear hands.

I'm astonished at all these hands that have touched.

Touching...

December 16

Gracious God,

There are days when I like to read some of my favorite quotes.

Usually when I do that, one jumps out and speaks to me in a special way.

Maybe Grandma has some favorite quotes and one will reach out and touch her today.

Igniting...

December 17

Faithful Father,

Does Grandma know how wealthy she really is?

I have an idea.

It seems that if Grandma were to write down a list
of riches she has that didn't cost any money,
she would be wonderfully surprised.

Awareness...

December 18

Magnificent Christ,

Would it be okay to do something fun?

The next time Grandma writes a letter would it
be okay for her to write it upside down?

You know if she's sending the letter in a card,
write on it upside down – just because.

Uncanny...

December 19

Enchanting Father,

Let's have a tea party with Grandma.

Maybe Grandma could take one of her
beautiful and special teacups and
have a spot of tea this afternoon.

Maybe while she sips her tea she can
pretend I'm there with her.

Soothing...

December 20

Festive Father,

It's time to sing!

Today when I thought about Grandma
I imagined that we were all bundled up with coats,
scarves, and gloves, and we were walking down the
streets of the place where she lives.

We're caroling.

And a small child heard us sing and a heart was opened.

Maybe Grandma is singing with me today.

Sing, sing, singing...

December 21

Calling on God! Calling on God!

I did something fun today.

I made a paper doll of my Grandma and dressed her
up in a dress with pokie dots and loud stripes.

I want to see this picture of my Grandma when
I open the refrigerator door.

When I see it, and smile and pretend I'm
talking with Grandma.

Playfully...

December 22

Buoyant God,

No matter where we might try to put you,
you always find a way to come to the surface.

I am grateful that you are up on the surface with Grandma.

You're like a big bubble that just can't stay
hidden or underneath something.

You always have to come up and make yourself known.

Trajectories...

December 23

Shhhh.

You hear that?

Hear that nothing sound?

Can you hear that there is quiet?

What peace will be Grandma's, dear God?

What quiet will befall her?

Silently...

December 24

Wow God!

It's the eve of Christmas.

There's excitement in the air!

Does Grandma, even now, still feel
like an excited child?

Does she sense the anticipation of
the birth of your son?

Does she tickle inside like a child
who's awaiting the sound of
reindeer on the rooftop?

Does she still leave a cookie and
milk out for Santa Clause?

Does she know you're there?

Eagerly...

December 25

Heavenly Father,

This is wonderment.

It feels different than other days.

Somehow people seem really focused
and it makes the world feel good.

Merry Christmas.

December 26

...Thank you.

December 27

Colorful Savior,

Do you suppose it would be okay for
Grandma to have nothing days?

Nothing days are when you let
yourself just sit if you want to.

Maybe take four naps instead of one.
Maybe your nothing day involves
coloring in a color book.

Maybe your nothing day means eating jello
whenever you want to and having as many
cups of hot chocolate as you can stand.

Nothing days refresh active days.

Experimenting...

December 28

Caring Father,

What am I going to do? What am I going to do?

How can I help Grandma today?

What would you have me do to provide
just what is needed?

Let her know that I'm here for her.

I'm sprinkling magical stardust and sending it her way.

Let the dust fall where it needs to so that
it's just right for Grandma.

Maybe I'll play for her.

December 29

Spirit of Joy.

This year is just about out of days!

Would it be okay to do something fun with Grandma?

I'm going to blow Grandma a kiss.
Would you be sure that she gets it?

One more thing. See me hugging myself?
I'm pretending that it's Grandma I'm hugging.

Would you be sure that she feels enveloped by my heart?

 Hugs and kisses, hugs and kisses, hugs and kisses...

December 30

Dear God,

I accept my Grandma just the way she is.

I love her.

She's the only Grandma I have
that is made just like she is.

What a marvelous gift.

Thank you for making her.

Thank you for watching over her.

Thank you for letting her receive
me as her grandchild.

Thank you for letting me be who I am with her.

Graciously...

December 31

Holy Father,

It's the last day of this year.

The year we've had is coming to a close and there is a new year knocking on the door.

Each day is a unique gift, as it is also a gift to be able to share a prayer with Grandma every day.

Thank you for hearing our prayers and for always being there to receive them and act on them.

In awe of your greatness...

Alexis Faere – Life Writes

Author, Blogger, Speaker, and Emotions Champion
AlexisFaere.com

Alexis Faere is an enchanting storyteller, writer, and whimsical spirit who weaves tales of magic and wonder. Her spiritual journey is shaped by her upbringing as a preacher's kid, where she quietly absorbed the profound truths and spiritual practices surrounding her daily life.

Today she shares her reflections and insights, offering these loving expressions to others, to deepen and strengthen a grandchild's connection with a grandparent. In addition to *Whispers of Love*, Alexis is the author of an insight-packed series of emotional journal workbooks, a blog (AlexisFaere.com), and soon-to-be-released memoir.

Whether she is penning a prayer or stories for adults or children, Alexis' words carry a timeless quality, resonating with readers of all ages. She invites readers on a transformative journey, drawing from her deep-rooted spirituality, personal reflections, and her passion to encourage emotional maturity and rich connections with people.

www.ingramcontent.com/pod-product-compliance
Lightning Source LLC
Chambersburg PA
CBHW080417030426
42335CB00020B/2482